Planting your Garden

A Wisley Gardening Companion

Planting your Garden

CHRISTOPHER LLOYD,
URSULA BUCHAN, FAY SHARMAN
and the Wisley Gardens Staff of
The Royal Horticultural Society

Cassell

The Royal Horticultural Society

THE ROYAL HORTICULTURAL SOCIETY

Cassell Educational Limited
Villiers House, 41/47 Strand
London WC2N 5JE
for the Royal Horticultural Society

First published 1993

British Library Cataloguing in Publication Data
A catalogue record for this book is available from the
British Library

ISBN 0–304–32043–9

Photographs by Eric Crichton, Valerie Finnis,
Andrew Lawson, Christopher Lloyd, Photos
Horticultural and Harry Smith Collection

Phototypesetting by RGM Associates, Southport

Printed in Hong Kong by Wing King Tong Co. Ltd.

Page 2: Clematis × jackmanii 'Superba' threaded through a
buddleia
Photograph by Photos Horticultural

Contents

Foreword

The first Wisley Handbooks, published in 1972, launched this most successful series, which has sold more than a million copies to date. From the beginning they have identified the subjects of most interest to the gardener. They originated as articles and lectures delivered to the Royal Horticultural Society, reprinted from the RHS *Journal*. One of the first pamphlets, *Hardy and Semi-Hardy Annuals in the Open Air*, sold for 2d. in 1915. Many of these early leaflets advised gardeners on wartime needs.

With the support and involvement of RHS staff as well as many other excellent authors, the Handbooks have always given clear and concise practical advice, ensuring their success. The first handbooks were 24 pages, stapled, with black and white illustrations. Now there are more than 60 Handbooks, each of 64 pages and illustrated in colour.

Here, *Planting your Garden* brings together four of the Handbooks, *The Mixed Border*, *Plants for Shade*, *Foliage Plants* and *Ground Cover Plants*, each contributing its personal mix of practical and sound information now contained in one volume.

Mixed borders allow one to enjoy the best features of different categories of plants which, when well chosen, provide a rich contrast of form, colour and height. Shade, often an integral part of the garden, can be a great asset and is enjoyed by the many plants suggested here. Foliage plants, those with interesting, unusual or beautiful leaves, are a perfect foil to colourful flowers and with the bonus of a longer season of interest. Ground cover plants have a spreading habit and form a canopy over the soil adding to the beauty of the garden and reducing the maintenance.

This volume will help you to choose the right plant for the right place – the aim of the Handbooks from the early days.

Christopher Brickell,
Director General,
The Royal Horticultural Society

Galanthus nivalis 'Sam Arnott', with large scented flowers, growing in the shade of a tree

The Mixed Border

— CHRISTOPHER LLOYD —

A soothing colour scheme using silver foliage and white- and blue-flowered plants, including delphiniums and nepeta

Introduction

The mixed border is the natural successor, in the evolution of garden history and practice, to the herbaceous border, to the border for annuals and tender plants, and to the shrubbery. Additionally, it gives us new scope for the use of bulbs.

Mankind has ever shown a tendency to categorise and pigeon-hole. This is natural when you are feeling your way into a new subject, and the experience of an individual is also the experience of a nation.

Coming fresh to gardening, you feel the need to anchor yourself to something; some flower, most likely. It may be roses. 'We must have a bed of roses', you'll say. Or of heathers or of conifers or perhaps, rather daringly for a beginner, of the two combined.

But when you mature, intellectually speaking, you come to realise that monocultures, though simple to grasp as a concept, are unnecessarily restrictive. To grow none but herbaceous plants together in a border, for instance, means that it will lack the substance and firmness of texture that could be introduced by shrubs, as it will also lack the continuity of colour provided by tender bedding plants. Why not enjoy the best features and examples of these different categories by combining them in a judicious mixture?

Opposite, top to bottom: Lupins interplanted with *Tulipa* 'Halcro', late May. Same view, mid-June, with lupins in flower. Lupins succeeded by *Malope trifida*, *Verbena bonariensis* in foreground, 21 October
Below: *Malope trifida*, showing green translucent calyx at flower base

Another and very practical advantage in the mixed border is that it avoids the dramatic build-up of pests and diseases that you will always find in monocultures. It is no accident that roses attract a longer list of these afflictions than any flower we grow. It is because so many of us are growing roses in gardens or beds devoted to them alone, that their pests and the pathogens causing their diseases can so easily build up to epidemic proportions. In a mixed border this can never happen. The pest that will attack one plant will find its neighbour distasteful. Roses are excellent mixed border plants. You'll not be able to grow so many of them as in a rose border but you will be able to grow a much wider variety of plants, and variety is truly the spice of life. The older I get the less I want to specialise, because specialisation is the enemy of variety with all its riches.

There is nothing new about the mixed border. Many of us have long been caring for or achieving one while calling it herbaceous. But in the long run the herbaceous border has earned itself a bad name as representing a singularly costly and lavish style of gardening that is closed to all but the rich (which generally means some public authority or institution, these days, caring for a historic garden like Hampton Court). I think it is the word herbaceous, in all its clumsiness, that puts people off the concept. Even if you drop the h, American style, and say 'erbaceous, you're no better off. And do you talk about an 'erbaceous border or a herbaceous border or a cross between the two? Many authors write an 'herbaceous border' but I doubt if they ever speak it like that.

Gertrude Jekyll never, in my reading of her, referred to her borders as herbaceous. 'I have a rather "mixed border of hardy flowers" ', she wrote in the late 1890s. 'It is not quite so hopelessly mixed as one generally sees, and the flowers are not all hardy.' That seems a pretty good mix to me.

A point worth remembering is that categories like shrub, herb, annual, biennial and bulb are merely terms coined for our own convenience. The plants themselves know nothing about them and often fall between two categories, in which case we need to compromise, rather lamely, by calling them sub-shrubs or short-lived perennials. We blithely classify cyclamen and anemones (some of them) as bulbs, but would leave out the agapanthus because it cannot be dried off and stored like other bulbs, although its close relationship to accredited bulbs like nerines, crinums and amaryllis is clear for all to see.

In nature, plants mix all the time, so why not in the garden? In a mature piece of woodland you'll find a tree canopy, a layer of shade-tolerating shrubs beneath that, and beneath them, again, herbs like trilliums, dog's-tooth violets, Virginian cowslips and anemones; plants which can complete all their flowering and

14

growing in the early months of the year when there is plenty of light reaching them and before the trees and shrubs have put on their leaves. There is much we can learn from this.

SIZE AND SHAPE

A border can be of any size or shape. The advantage of plots that are freely intersected by paths is that you can reach every plant without stepping on the border. For a cottage-style garden this works well enough but my own recommendation would be to make, where given the opportunity, one large border in preference to several small ones. It means that you can use larger growing plants without upsetting the balance. Tall plants look ridiculous in a small border. It also means that you have scope for grouping some of your plants, which looks so much more effective than dotting them singly all over the place. This is the cottage garden tendency; one that can look charming, but is often a fidgety mess that allows the eye nowhere to rest.

Another fidget to avoid – yet how frequently you see it – is a fussy outline to a border. Where you use curves make them long, smooth and easy, not short, crimped and wiggly. Curves should appear inevitable and not to have been made for their own sake in an 'I love curves' orgy. Straight lines within a formal or architectural setting will often look appropriate and are nothing to be ashamed of. Your plants themselves can break up the line of a hard edge by lapping over it.

YOUR BORDER'S SEASON

A shrub like a yucca can look pretty good (if you like it in the first place) at all times of the year, but most plants have a seasonal peak, outside which they are at best inoffensive but still mere passengers. Others, in their dormant period or when we are tired of them, disappear from the scene altogether.

When planning a bed – and it is always better planned than tumbled into – you should have a definite peak season in mind, during which none of the contents is looking sordid or disreputable.

Let us say (as I choose to make it) that this period is from mid-June to mid-August. That's two months, and to expect longer at high pressure is both greedy and unpractical. But you can, as I shall show, include earlier interest without diluting the main impact and you can also do much to prolong the display into autumn.

There are so many plants to choose from that it is a positive advantage to impose restrictions on ourselves in one way or another. One such is that a plant's season of beauty should not be

Early June, with pink *Weigela florida* 'Variegata', Dickson's golden elm behind

too short. I will take *Lychnis chalcedonica*, sometimes called the Maltese cross, on account of the notch at the tip of each petal, as an example. This 3–4 ft (90 cm–1.2 m) hardy perennial carries domed heads of pure scarlet in July. It is a rare and, to those not frightened of handling it, an invaluable colour to find in a perennial at this season (it occurs in the oriental poppy a month earlier). The snag is that it lasts a mere two weeks, and whatever treatment you give the plant afterwards, it will have nothing more to offer. In a large border you can accommodate a few, but only a few, passengers like this. You could plant in front of it a later developer like *Verbena bonariensis* or *Cimicifuga racemosa*, which would raise itself above lychnis level after the latter had made its bow.

Such problems and working out the best solutions are the very stuff of creative gardening and only next in importance to growing a plant well in the first place.

There are some devices for prolonging a border's season which are perfectly simple; other that are labour intensive in the extreme. Most popular writing on our subject today concentrates on labour saving (low maintenance, the Americans call it), and that's fair

16

Late August, *Crocosmia* 'Citronella' in front of weigela, *Aster sedifolius* (*A. acris*) left, *Salix alba* 'Argentea' with elm

enough when you are addressing reluctant garden owners. But we are a nation of gardeners such as exists nowhere else in the world and we have the best of all climates for our purpose. So it is nothing to apologise for if we enjoy labour when it is productive of something rather special.

Suppose you had a sitting out area and, behind that, a window to look from in less clement weather. Your view might well be of a mixed border designed in a broad, curving sweep with a hedge or evergreen shrubs behind it to form a background. I would still recommend that you aim at a limited season for that border's peak, but I would also suggest that you stick at nothing to prolong it by all manner of 'cheating' (as some would describe it but I'm not about to recommend plastic flowers or celluloid models of pink flamingoes), especially if you have a back-up area in the way of spare ground, a greenhouse or cold frames in which to keep plants in reserve until they are needed.

Patches of early flowering annuals in your border could then be replaced by others, moved in at the critical moment from the reserve. And not only annuals. Perennials like doronicums,

Achillea 'Moonshine' or *A.* × *taygetea*, pyrethrums, epimediums, astilbes or anything else with an easy-going, fibrous root system, can be moved to a spare row after flowering and be replaced for a late summer and autumn display by other perennials of a similar root system. Such are *Aster* × *frikartii*, *A. amellus* and all the traditional michaelmas daisies; similarly chrysanthemums of the Korean and other sufficiently early flowering types. Perennial lobelias (*L. fulgens*, *L. cardinalis*, *L. vedrariensis*, *L. syphilitica* and cultivars derived from them) are good movers even as late as August, when coming into flower. Hebes move beautifully and especially suitable are the most glamorously flowering but somewhat tender kinds like 'Andersonii Variegata', 'Simon Delaux', 'Evelyn' and 'La Séduisante'. Theirs is a 3 to 4-months-long season, particularly if you snap the dead spikes off as they run to seed. There are many other possibilities and you can experiment for yourself.

The one essential for success is to do the job properly. This, in most weathers, will entail a heavy watering the day before moving of everything that's to be moved, whether into or out of your border, followed by a further liberal watering after planting, to settle them in. If, at this stage, the water is liable to pan the surface and run off it, I prefer to puddle the plants in. That is to say, I dig my hole, set the plant in it, pour over its roots anything up to a gallon of water, quickly from an upturned watering can, and then, as that is draining but not quite drained away, scoop in the soil to fill the hole.

Such practices sound like and are a lot of work; interesting work but undeniably time and effort consuming. So to the question which will be put sooner rather than later 'are mixed borders labour saving?', the answer is that they can be, but that the greater the inputs the greater the outputs. The most sensible course to adopt is to use some plants that will do the work for you by covering the ground, suppressing weeds and looking mildly agreeable over a long season. The time thus saved can then the more willingly be devoted to other plants which will yield even greater rewards, but only if you take trouble over them. The balance can be tilted one way or the other according to how well you are feeling, how keen on the garden, how involved in other matters and what help you can muster.

THE SITE

A site open to sunshine (given our climate) but protected from wind, is to be preferred. However, there are many shade loving plants, so long as it is not the dense, dry, rooty shade brooded over by trees like beech or cherry. Few plants worth having will grow happily under them and it is certainly no place to start a mixed border.

Wind protection is not essential but makes life more comfortable for you as well as for the plants. On a windy site you must use lower growing plants. Those with grey felted leaves are particularly well adapted to wind, if it is not icy from the north or east.

A southerly aspect is ideal for a one-sided border. Its background, whether wall, fence, hedge or shrubs, will protect it from the coldest winds. A north-facing border can be managed but the chief disadvantage, since it will be viewed from the north, is that all the plants will be leaning and, in many cases, turning their leaves and flowers towards the south. In those that are anyway shade loving like nicotianas, busy lizzies, begonias, cimicifugas, border phloxes, ferns, fatsia and aucuba, this would not be noticed. It's a matter of making the right choices.

There is no question of aspect for an island bed that receives ample light from every direction. The main problem here is backgrounds dark enough to highlight the flowers. These backgrounds can, if sufficiently tall, as on rising ground, be at a considerable distance from the border they are highlighting.

Paved or other hard margins to your borders will be the most satisfying, as they'll allow the pool and cushion forming plants to spread forward in a pleasantly relaxed manner during their growing season, which also effectively adds to the width of a border. I personally feel no scruples about allowing my plants to lap on to a lawn in summer, as I loathe the cliff-like edge and sterilely empty strip of earth that prim-minded gardeners enforce between a lawn and the first plants in a border. Plants don't seem to be enjoying themselves under this regime and I cannot enjoy them. You can perfectly well manage the lawn grass next to an overlapping plant, if you want to, and the bare patch left by the plant at the end of the growing season will soon fill in, even if only with annual meadow grass. Lawns should be considered an adjunct to borders and not an end in themselves.

PREPARATIONS FOR A NEW BORDER

Never be in a hurry when making a new border. Adverse basic factors are far easier to remedy before it has been planted, so you may well need to allow a year, which will include an entire growing season, in which to make ready. But I am not about to recommend double digging. That is quite unnecessary.

Good drainage even in the wettest weather is all-important. Plants can't swim and they can all too easily drown. If in any doubt, lay tile drains and don't put them in too deep, otherwise the water

that is afflicting your plants may never reach the drains. They need be no deeper than 12–15 in. (30–38 cm), which is below the depth you'll want to dig in the course of ordinary cultivations.

If the garden adjoins a recently completed house, the chances are that the builders will have dumped the subsoil from their excavations on top of the natural soil in your garden. Nothing will grow in subsoil. It must be removed. If the garden needs landscaping, then its top soil must be set on one side while the alterations are made, and returned at the end. It is often desirable to bring in additional top soil from another building site, with which to make good your own losses.

What kind of soil are you dealing with? If light, it will have the advantage that you can do what you like on it half an hour after heavy rains at any season of the year. It will drain easily and be easy to work. But it will dry out quickly and will probably be short of water-retentive organic matter. You'll need to add this, right through the border's life, in generous quantities. Rather coarse sedge peat has excellent physical properties. So has bark, but if this is fresh it should be stacked for a year before use, otherwise it takes nitrogen from the soil in the course of decomposition and will thus deprive your plants. It's the same story with any raw organic

Opposite: *Geranium psilostemon* supported by *Crambe cordifolia*, with spikes of foxglove and mullein
Above: *Geranium endressii* 'Claridge Druce' mingles with *Cornus alba* 'Elegantissima'
Below: *Geranium sanguineum* knits into pale yellow *Achillea* × *taygetea*

matter. Farmyard manure, if it smells ammoniacal, is still not ready for use on ground that is shortly to be, or has already been, planted. But you can dig it into a border in autumn that will not be planted until the next year. Well decayed garden compost is good and there are a number of other possibilities according to availability in the area where you live.

Heavy soils are water retentive which is a good thing if you have their drainage under control. You can permanently improve their physical properties by the addition of large quantities of grit, which is crushed shingle and is of a coarser texture than any natural sand. Spread it so thickly that, before digging it in, the soil beneath is invisible. You may have difficulty in finding a supplier in your locality; builders' merchants are the best bet. Fertility, as always, will be improved by the addition of decayed organic matter, which is humus.

If weeds, especially docks and nettles, are growing luxuriantly on your plot when you come to it, this is a good sign and indicates high fertility, without which you will never be successful, but you must get rid of them all the same. Indeed, you must make sure of having wiped out all perennial weeds in a border before you start to plant it up, otherwise their recurrence from dormant roots will give you endless trouble. When these weeds are growing strongly, treat them with glyphosate, which is marketed as Roundup (wholesale) or Tumbleweed (retail). It is non-residual in the soil but systemic in the plants treated, destroying their roots as well as the visible portions sprayed. A second application may be necessary in the case of very persistent weeds like ground elder.

Immediately prior to planting (generally in autumn or spring but there is no dead season, except as imposed by the weather) get the top soil into a friable condition that will make it easy to settle around plant roots. You can either fork it over, breaking lumps down with the back of your fork as you go, or you can use a mechanical cultivator.

If you are planting to a scale plan, you'll need to transfer it to the border with the help of a string grid, thereafter marking in the outline plants with a cane and a label. Or you may prefer to work on an ad hoc basis, having collected a reservoir of plants in a spare plot during the months or year in which you were making the site ready.

With an original plan you'll make fewer mistakes in the first instance, because you'll have had time to work out colour juxta-positions and relative plant heights but you'll make plenty of mistakes however you set about it. The great thing is not to mind admitting them and to change things round when you see what's wrong. All gardening involves constant change and your border should never be complete but always in a state of evolution.

Do make groups as well as planting singletons, especially in the first instance, when you're starting with empty ground and you're not yet cramped for space in which to grow all the treasures you long to possess. Even with shrubs, a group of something like *Potentilla fruticosa*, *Caryopteris* or *Perovskia* will look the more effective for not just being dotted around. With plants, even more so. A single phlox is meaningless. You need to see a mass of it to create a plushy impression. The same with cushions of *Sedum* 'Autumn Joy' or *S. spectabile*.

RESTRICTIONS ON PLANT CHOICE

I have already pointed out the joy of there being so few restrictions imposed upon you as to what you may grow in a mixed border. Even cacti (some opuntias are hardy) can be included if they appeal to you.

But there are certain limitations imposed from without and others by personal choice and preference.

From without, climate, soil and availability are the most obvious. The foliage shrub, *Gleditsia triacanthos* 'Sunburst', which I grow in a mixed border in Sussex would not thrive for anyone north of the midlands. Its young wood does not ripen enough in the summer to carry it through the following winter. Similarly there are autumn flowering plants, like certain pampas grasses, that do not develop their flowers in time before the growing season comes to an end, while the wood of *Camellia japonica* cultivars is apt not to ripen sufficiently, given cool summers, to bud up well for next spring's flowering. These are typical climate limitations.

In respect of soil, the most obvious and best known is the fact that on alkaline (limy, chalky) soils, such plants as rhododendrons, camellias, many meconopses and heathers will not grow. Others, like hydrangeas, will develop bright yellow foliage and not grow too well, though it may be possible to keep them happy by applying regular doses of iron Sequestrene. On the whole it is sensible (and dignified) to grow the plants that your soil suits (there'll always be plenty of them) and not wring your hands over the rest.

Another big moan is always sent up when a plant that you have read about in the press is not available from your local garden centre. There's no such thing as an unobtainable plant, but you have to search around (for pity's sake enclose a stamped, addressed envelope when badgering someone with enquiries). If you join an organisation like the Hardy Plant Society, you'll be in on plant and seed exchanges of rare items. If you're a member of the Royal Horticultural Society, it will help if it can. But if a plant remains unobtainable for the time being, console yourself with the thought

23

that your border can only accommodate a tiny fraction of the vast number that *are* available.

For this reason it may sometimes please you to impose your own restrictions, the commonest being to limit the flower and plant colours in your border. All-grey-and-white is very popular, with a bow towards Sissinghurst Castle as the fashionable prototype. Some people are crazy on blue flowers. Unfortunately they usually mix in those with mauve and purple in their make-up and this is a mismatch. Blue anyway looks rather dead on its own and is much livelier when combined with yellow or pink or white. All-yellow borders look good and can include plenty of variegated foliage. Many gardeners are nervous of misusing yellow, in case it clashes unacceptably with bright pink or magenta. All-yellow is a way out of this, but yellow and white is even better, I think.

For myself, I am happy with a complete mixture, though I do watch what's going immediately next to what. The bright pink of rose 'Zéphirine Drouhin' will look happier next to spikes of blue delphiniums than in the company of a yellow daisy like *Buphthalmum (Telekia) speciosum.*

A MIXED BORDER IN MATURITY

Before going on to consider the different types of plants used in mixed borders in greater detail, I will make some general remarks on upkeep.

It will never be necessary, unless you have allowed the weed problem to get out of control, to take everything out of the border and start again, as is the routine recommended for herbaceous borders every 6 years or so.

All work in a mixed border will be on a piecemeal basis. Where perennials are in question, organise matters so that they don't all reach the stage of needing to be divided and re-set simultaneously. Otherwise your border will look weak in the following summer.

But I like to go right through a border, examining and, if necessary, attending to its components once a year. The main time for this can be in autumn or in spring. I used to be an autumn over-hauler but now prefer spring – March, to wit. The days, then, are not so aggravatingly short as in autumn and perhaps you are, on average, less frequently interrupted by rain. Also you can see where the bulbs are and avoid them. Herbaceous rubbish that you carry away is paper light by then.

To leave certain plants that will eventually need cutting right down looking derelict until the spring may be a worry, especially if your border is constantly within your sight lines. Mine is not and I'm quite well trained, by now, not to notice what I don't want to see, but only in the dormant season when the garden is little frequented. And many skeletons that look derelict at one moment may suddenly be transformed by frost or snow into objects of beauty.

One of the advantages of the mixed border in winter is the variety of shapes and colours that it still retains at that season, even when there's no flower to be seen.

Whether you cut your plants down in autumn or in spring, I would advise you never to do it until you are ready to deal with that piece of ground – weeding, planting, splitting, dividing and replanting or whatever. It is far easier to remember how your plants grew; indeed, to remember what they are, while their skeletons are before you. You also need to recollect how they stood in relation to one another. You can act logically only if you know these things. Furthermore, the ground beneath plants that have not been cut down is largely protected from the slimy conditions imposed by rain and frost. Deal with a little stretch of border at a time; then another stretch. Finish each stretch before the night's rain or frost sets in.

The time for the pruning, thinning or trimming of shrubs will vary but it is often possible to get on with some of this, like the pollarding of willows or the cutting back of some other foliage shrub such as the golden cut-leaved elder, in the depths of winter when the ground is too hard for planting, weeding or cultivating. Where I live I like to prune my roses in winter too. With most of them it is principally a question of thinning out old branches.

While the ground is still wet, you should apply your surface, moisture-retaining mulches, whether of decayed leaves, peat, bark, garden compost or whatever. In March, we put on a surface dressing of chicken manure well decayed in sawdust. We have a deep litter chicken house, from which this comes. As this manure is always kept under cover until actually used, it is rich in nutrients but devoid of weed seeds, which is a great advantage. Even so we add a balanced dressing of general fertilizer at this season, containing nitrogen, phosphorus and potassium, at 4oz to the square yard. This gives the newly growing plants a boost. You may prefer a slower-acting organic fertilizer like hoof-and-horn. My chicken manure is the slow-acting side of it.

By May, some of your plants will need supporting. If the site is really open, you will require more support but the plants less. The irony of this situation is explained by the fact of an open, sunny situation inducing stocky, wind resistant growth. In sheltered and particularly in one-sided borders, the plants become drawn. Still, it's usually the best way to give them a background and this is therefore a situation to be tolerated.

25

Always leave enough space – say 15 in. (38 cm) – between groups of plants in a border, to allow you to move between them without leaving a trail of damage. This will not prevent the foliage from joining up between groups. The indecency of earth visible in high summer should never be tolerated, but that is no excuse for congested planting.

How you support your plants will partly depend on what you can find. We use hornbeam or hazel peasticks for such as monarda, *Salvia nemorosa* 'Superba', *Alstroemeria ligtu* hybrids and *Aster sedifolius* (*A. acris*). But you could make a job of it with canes and a cat's cradle of fillis, which is soft, fawn-coloured string, stretched between canes, starting and finished with a clove hitch. Five-ply fillis is the right strength to last a season in most cases.

I always use the canes and fillis technique with stemmier plants such as *Achillea filipendulina*, *Aconitum* 'Sparks' and the tall wild prototype of *Phlox paniculata*. With a clump of delphiniums you can usually get by with a triangle of canes (knock them in *straight* and with the broad end *downwards*), passing the fillis with a twist around each delphinium stem on the way to hitching it at each cane. Wait till you can do this at the 3–4 ft (90 cm–1.2 m) level and you'll only need the one tie, using strong, 5 ft (1.5 m) canes. Real heavies like the flowering stems of cardoon, *Cynara cardunculus*, need chestnut posts and telephone cables (or a heavy grade of tarred string) for support.

Dead-heading of spent blooms continues right through the summer and into autumn. Conscientiously pursued, it makes all the difference to a border's appearance as the season progresses. Never dead-head to leave a projecting piece of stem. Cut back almost flush with the base of a leaf or pair of leaves.

With some flowers you dead-head in the expectation of a second crop to follow; for instance *Salvia* 'Superba' (more persistent than any of the dwarf cultivars), early flowering phloxes and heleniums, *Anthemis tinctoria*. When a low plant like *Viola cornuta*, *Geranium sanguineum*, giant chives (*Allium*) or *Alchemilla mollis* looks spent and tatty, cut it all to the ground, give it a dose of fertilizer and water heavily.

In other cases, and with shrubs like summer flowering buddleias, the Jerusalem sage (*Phlomis fruticosa*) and *Senecio* 'Sunshine', the dead-heading is a mere tidying up procedure.

Meantime the process of rejuvenating certain areas in the border can go right into late August or early September with the introduction of chrysanthemum and michaelmas daisy plants.

The time has come to consider the kinds of plants suitable for mixed borders in greater detail.

A truly mixed border, with herbaceous plants for foliage and flower, shrubs and trees, photographed in June

Elaeagnus commutata with its white oval leaves dominates this border.
This deciduous shrub may grow to 10 ft (3 m)

Shrubs

Two kinds of shrubs can be distinguished for our purpose. There are those which build up a permanent framework and comprise backbone elements. They develop a structure and give body to a planting which can be appreciated and enjoyed in winter as well as summer.

Second, there are those whose growth we restrict by hard pruning every year and which therefore develop little more personality than does a herbaceous plant. That, in its peak season, can be considerable but in winter it is nothing. These are shrubs that we grow for their late summer flowers or for foliage effect. I'll take the first group first.

STRUCTURAL SHRUBS

Most such flower on the wood they made in the previous year and they do so in the following spring; at latest, as with *Philadelphus*, by mid-July. The vast majority of flowering shrubs belong to spring. If our border aims, as it probably will do, at a summer season, such shrubs will be a drug on the market. They will be so many lumps of greenery.

This is not to say that a mixed border specialising in an April-May season could not be made. The foliage of many hostas is at its freshest then. Perennials with an early flowering season would be included near the border's margin, for most such are short-stemmed. There would be dicentras and early primulas; doronicums, omphalodes and brunneras. Many such plants are tolerant of shade, so they could run into the shrub plantings. There would be globe flowers, the double white *Ranunculus aconitifolius* as well as other double buttercups. Forget-me-nots could be allowed to self-sow and there would be the big white violet, *Viola cucullata* as well as smaller drift-forming kinds like the yellow *V. biflora* and the purple *V. labradorica* which also has purple leaves and shows up so well with that low-growing evergreen shrub *Euonymus fortunei* 'Green-'n-Gold'. Given reasonable moisture, ferns could run in and out of the shrubs, particularly the shuttlecock, *Matteuccia struthiopteris*; the sensitive, *Onoclea sensibilis*, and the oak, *Gymnocarpium dryopteris*, all of remarkable freshness in the early part of their season.

There would be little scope for annuals, perhaps, but of biennials the lime green, parsley-like inflorescences and conspicuous bracts of *Smyrnium perfoliatum* would be particularly at home as also the various strains of honesty, *Lunaria annua*, of which the pure white form shows up best beneath shrub shade.

Bulbs would be there in force, though I should tend to avoid the largest and most lumpish tulips and daffodils. The latters' leaves die off particularly obtrusively in May. Erythroniums would be absolutely right as also the rhizomatous anemones such as *Anemone apennina*. Once established, *Cyclamen repandum* can make a splendid colony beneath shrubs.

All this would make an exciting exercise and to get the balance right I think you should actually lay emphasis on the herbs and bulbs and not yield to the temptation of allowing azaleas and other rhododendrons (assuming that your soil is acid enough to grow them), camellias, viburnums, corylopsis, barberries, spiraeas and the rest of them become too dominant. Remember that spring-flowering herbs, bulbs and the plants like hostas, rodgersias and ferns grown for their foliage, have a much better chance to develop well among and, even more so, underneath deciduous shrubs, which cast little shade until late May, than among evergreens.

An early-season mixed border such as this would carry little interest beyond May. A garden needs to be fairly large for the owners to be prepared to turn their backs on a major feature from June onwards, just when we expect to enjoy living in the open most. It is short-sighted to allow ourselves to be dominated by the spring garden. A rule of thumb that I have found to work well for me is to concentrate, in my planning, on the summer and autumn scene. Spring, with all the freshness of foliage which turns the whole countryside into something as beguiling as any garden, has a way of looking after itself.

So I will return to my original concept of a mixed border that concentrates on the mid-June to mid-August period, but encourages foretastes and aftermaths insofar as these do not detract from the main season.

Viburnum opulus 'Compactum', for instance, gets in on the basis of flowering prettily with white lacecaps in May, but more importantly, of already ripening its clusters of gleaming red berries in August and these hang on for several months without attracting the birds (don't ask me why). This is a less voluminous version of our native guelder rose, but it does need quite careful pruning both to reduce its bulk and to promote a steady flow of flowers and fruit without these becoming a biennial feature with no contribution in the off years. Come the winter, when your shrub is naked and can be properly seen, remove some of the most heavily fruited branches and leave those that have quite a lot of young wood on them and will flower and fruit for you on this in the next season.

Mahonia 'Undulata' is a shrub that I give space to, even though it flowers in April. Its glossy, wavy-margined leaves are particularly smart, and they change to sumptuous purple in the cold winter's weather. Even so, it must not occupy as much space as it would like, and I cut it hard back into old wood every fifth spring.

Weigela florida 'Variegata' is not a wonderful shrub, structurally, however well you prune it, and its flowering season – a mass of scented, pale pink trumpets – in May, is well outside our requirements. But its foliage, first green and white, then green and yellow, is a meal in itself and makes a wonderful background to bronze or red flowers, as it might be heleniums or dahlias.

The Mount Etna broom, *Genista aetnensis*, is a case of its own. It is the longest lived of all the brooms (mine is now 35 years old and still going strong) and it eventually becomes a small tree, 15 ft (4.5 m) or more high, but because its growth is so light and airy, making virtually no foliage, it never becomes overbearing. So much light penetrates its branches that you can plant underneath with other summer flowerers. Its own season, when it is a fountain of tiny yellow, scented blossom, is July-August.

Of the structural shrubs that you plant in a mixed border, I should warn that they are often slow growing in youth (structure takes time to build up) compared with their flimsy annual, biennial or herbaceous perennial neighbours. The latter can easily shade them out, in these early years, and this requires preventative vigilance on your part.

SHRUBS FOR SUMMER–AUTUMN FLOWERING OR FOR FOLIAGE EFFECT

These shrubs, in the main, make their display, whether of flowers or of foliage, on young shoots of the current season's growth. They therefore lend themselves to a hard annual cutting back. This, it will be observed, is the same treatment as we give to hardy perennials, the only difference being that in the one case we cut to the ground, in the other to a stool, stump or lowish framework. The annual habit of growth, in each case, is very similar, which makes this type of shrub particularly well suited to the company of perennials. Their needs are the same.

Cultivars of the butterfly bush, *Buddleia davidii*, are the best known example. Of the shrub *Hypericum*, 'Hidcote' is familiar with its flat saucers of yellow flowers. Richer coloured and more deeply cupped is 'Rowallane', but it is slightly less hardy. The summer flowering tamarisk, *Tamarix ramosissima* (better known as *T. pentandra*), produces a haze of pink spikelets in a gauze of pale green foliage. You can cut it back in winter to a 2–3 ft (60–90 cm) stump. It looks well, in its season, behind *Verbena bonariensis* or next to the tall white *Cimicifuga racemosa*.

The scented Spanish broom, *Spartium junceum*, flowers in yellows spikelets at the tips of its young shoots, and looks well with something white, as it might be a *Philadelphus* or rose 'Iceberg'. Many fuchsias are remarkably hardy, but mostly respond best to being cut to the ground each early spring. The red and purple 'Mrs Popple' looks well, at 3 ft (90 cm), with the somewhat taller, pale pink *Abelia* × *grandiflora*. Both have a long season.

Blue-flowered shrubs are all too rare but such are the hardy plumbago *Ceratostigma willmottianum* (another good partner for red fuchsias), *Caryopteris* × *clandonensis*, of which the most intensively coloured clones are 'Ferndown', 'Kew Blue' and 'Heavenly Blue'; and *Perovskia atriplicifolia*, with branching panicles of sage-like flowers on upright 3–4 ft (90 cm–1.2 m) stems.

Romneya, the Californian tree poppy, responds to being cut absolutely to ground level in winter, at which time it can take turns with a dazzling display of winter aconites (*Eranthis*) and *Crocus tommasinianus* (with variations at your pleasure). Floppy white, yellow-stamened poppies are borne at 6 ft (1.8 m) in July-August above grey foliage. This plant spreads by suckering and will take up quite a lot of space. So does and will *Sambucus canadensis* 'Maxima', an elder that flowers on its young wood with enormous corymbs, a foot or more across.

Among hydrangeas, the ultra-hardy kinds that flower on their young shoots and respond to a hard winter cut back, are all white. *Hydrangea paniculata* has a cone-shaped inflorescence, and is most popular in the cultivar 'Grandiflora', wherein the florets are all of the large, sterile kind and make a heavy head. It fades to pink. More elegant are 'Tardiva' and 'Floribunda' (the difference between them eludes me), in which the large sterile florets are interspersed with a fuzz of tiny fertile ones. In *H. arborescens* 'Grandiflora' (another heavy-headed but excellent clone) and *H. a. discolor* 'Sterilis', the inflorescence is globular. These look smashing with border phloxes, cultivars of *Phlox paniculata*, and both will put up with quite a bit of shade. Another good partner for the July-flowering 'Sterilis' is the spiky yellow loosestrife, *Lysimachia punctata*.

Other hydrangeas, whether lacecaps or hortensias (flat-headed or bun-shaped) are first rate mixed border ingredients and they are generally coloured, but their pruning is not of the cutting back type. In March you should remove 3 to 4-year-old branches that have become weakened by flowering, either completely, right back to ground level (a narrow-bladed saw helps you to get really low among a forest of stems) or back to a strong, unbranched young shoot if such occurs in its lower regions. In this way you thin out and let light into a bush, which itself encourages the production of new growth in the next season and renews the entire bush over a period of four years or so. Generous feeding in spring should go with this treatment.

Hydrangeas look well in groups and, being deciduous, lend themselves to underplanting with early bulbs. One of the most effective in a mixed border setting is 'Preziosa' (derived from *H. serrata*) with small bun heads of sterile florets that start pale pink but gradually change to deep ruby red (purple, on acid soil). The leaves and young stems are attractively flushed red. It has a long season because new flower heads keep developing. This is also a main asset in 'Générale Vicomtesse de Vibraye', a hortensia which is probably at its most alluring on acid soil, when the colouring is light blue. It is one of the hardiest.

Quite different are the large shrubs with felted leaves made by *H. sargentiana* and *H. villosa*. Both are winter hardy but subject to serious damage by spring frosts on their young shoots. They also need wind shelter to prevent bruising of their large leaves in summer. In *H. sargentiana* these may, in a shady situation, be 15 in. (38 cm) long by 9 in. (23 cm) across. The lacecap flower heads with a ring of sterile florets surrounding a platform of tiny fertile flowers, are pale mauve. The colouring is a rich shade of lilac in the sterile florets of *H. villosa*, while the central flowers are blue. In its August season this is the most beautiful flower in my garden. There is a dense carpet beneath it of *Saxifraga × geum*, whose mist of tiny blush flowers appears in May.

The best known and perhaps the showiest *Indigofera* is *I. heterantha*, with axillary spikelets of deep rosy mauve pea flowers. You can keep this to a low framework or cut it to the ground, if you prefer, in which case it will not exceed 3–4 ft (90 cm–1.2 m).

There are some rather more substantial late flowering shrubs that do not demand hard pruning. Most are white-flowered, which is curious. Some useful privet species come into this category, in particular the August-September *Ligustrum quihoui*, which is peculiarly elegant with narrow leaves and long sprays of blossom. Pruning consists of removing flowered shoots in winter, leaving the unflowered wands intact. *Ligustrum × vicaryi* is July-flowering and also carries handsome crops of black berries. Its evergreen leaves are lime green. Again, remove flowered and fruited branches to prune.

Eucryphias have white summer flowers with many stamens. *Eucryphia glutinosa* is the hardiest, a deciduous shrub, colouring well in the autumn. 'Nymansay' will make a tree in time but can be kept to a narrow spire, with a little help. Its bold flowers open in August and are a workshop for bees. It will tolerate some lime, which *E. glutinosa* does not.

Hoheria glabrata and *H. lyallii* are similar and often muddled, which doesn't really matter. Both are fast growing shrubs in the mallow family with heart-shaped leaves and masses of white, scented blossom (not unlike a cherry's in general effect) in July.

The great merit of foliage shrubs in a mixed border is the tremendous value they give – year-round in some cases. My biggest feature would be a tree. Dickson's golden elm (*Ulmus* 'Dicksonii', of uncertain parentage), with its bright lime green colouring, makes a yellow impression which lasts the season through. It looks all the better for clipping (done every other year) because the leaves on the young shoots rise vertically in two ranks and overlap like feathers. A pale silver-grey willow in front makes a telling contrast: our native white willow *Salix alba* in a less vigorous but whiter form, 'Argentea'. It receives an annual pollarding in winter. To complete the mixed border image, I have established a handsome parasite on its roots (from a lump of soil containing its own roots), *Lathraea clandestina*. Entirely leafless, its bright purple, hooded flowers appear in dense clusters just above ground level in March and continue flowering till May. There are also scented violets, some pink, some purple, beneath these shrubs.

It is a holly, *Ilex × altaclerensis* 'Golden King', filling the back corner of my mixed border, that gives greatest year-round pleasure. It is almost prickle-free (which makes a lot of difference when you're grubbing about for weeds), with a golden leaf margin. It berries freely almost every year. Although slow growing it is the better for clipping over by hand every 5 or 6 years, so as to retain a dense habit.

Lonicera nitida 'Baggesen's Gold' I clip every year in February, just as growth is starting up. It looks awful at first but soon takes on a more relaxed appearance and if you don't do this the plant soon becomes scrawny. Its yellow-green colouring looks well in conjunction with *Cotinus coggygria* in its purple (but greenish purple, not purple purple) form, 'Purpurea', which also makes masses of purplish 'smoke' on the inflorescence. The deep 'Notcutt's Variety' and the even richer 'Royal Purple' do not do this.

If you want 'Purpurea' to flower, prune selectively in winter, leaving those young shoots you wish to flower unpruned. If pruning entirely for foliage effect, as with 'Royal Purple', you can shorten the shoots all over. However, this weakens the shrub if done severely every year, so every other is generally the best compromise. A purple cotinus behind a deep pink phlox looks good in sunshine, or with the lime green blossom of *Alchemilla mollis* in front of it. Another telling combination is of the purple continus planted with the brilliantly glaucous foliage of *Eucalyptus gunnii*, itself stooled (i.e. cut back to a low stump) every or every other year. This promotes the disc-like juvenile foliage, which is the brightest and prettiest.

Another purple-leaved shrub (dusky mauve, really, with glaucous hints) that combines well with the eucalyptus is *Rosa glauca* (*R. rubrifolia*) grown entirely for foliage. To this end you cut back annually. You should also grow a plant more naturally for its modest but engaging flowers and its clusters of showy hips. From these you will find yourself the owner of self-sown seedlings, which you can then assemble into a group, planted 2–3 ft (60–90 cm) apart, and give them the foliage treatment.

Among the most silvery of grey-leaved shrubs is *Santolina pinnata neapolitana*, paler, with a longer leaf and more open-textured than the better known lavender cotton. Flowering is to the detriment of a foliage shrub like this. You prevent it and also promote a close-textured habit by cutting back to a low, woody stump each spring; spring, not winter, in cases like this where there is an element of doubt about hardiness. Even hardier, however, yet fulfilling the same function, a mound of grey at the 18 in. (45 cm) level, is *Helichrysum splendidum*. This is a stiffer shrub. It looks well in front of the feathery-textured conifer, *Chamaecyparis thyoides* 'Ericoides', which is sea green in summer, purple in winter.

Excellent grey value also from the comb leaves of *Artemisia* 'Powis Castle', 2 ft (60 cm) tall and of a spreading habit. It does not worry you by flowering and looking patchy. By the same token it needs less pruning. *Senecio cineraria* (*Cineraria maritima*) demands a hard spring cut-back. It has felted, pinnate leaves, whitest in 'White Diamond', most cut in 'Ramparts'. If you have a group of these you can interplant them with dwarf tulips, which will do their stuff while the shrub is in its reduced, cut-back phase. All this is at the border's margin, as we're talking in terms of 12–18 in. (30–45 cm) tall plants.

The most beautiful of all foliage plants that you can grow as hardy (if you're careful) is the South African *Melianthus major*, with sizeable, wax-smooth pinnate leaves, glaucous and with

35

Opposite: Pale yellow pansies and lilac scabious backed by artemisia, hebe, foxgloves and spiraea
Above: The mixed colours of a small garden in early summer

sharply toothed margins that cast shadows on the leaf surface when the sun is low. Although a shrub, you treat it as a herbaceous perennial, cutting its old stems (whether live or dead) down in spring. Meantime, in winter, you should pack fern fronds between them and cover the crowns, as a protection. Once established, the roots go deep, the shoots also appearing from quite deep down in spring, and you'll never lose it.

A Japanese maple is unlikely to be good material for a mixed border since it grows too slowly in the early years to compete with lush neighbours; otherwise I would certainly include *Acer japonicum* 'Aureum'. But the same colouring can be had on the large pinnate leaves of the golden cut-leaved elder, *Sambucus racemosa* 'Plumosa Aurea' and this, cut down to stumps in winter, will make 4 ft (1.2 m) of growth in a season. Like many golden leaved plants it tends to scorch in hot sunlight, especially if the soil is dry. Dense shade, on the other hand, will result in too green a colouring. Part shade is the right compromise.

There are a few trees or shrubs from which you can obtain enormous leaves by dint of cutting them to the ground each winter and then allowing only a few shoots per plant to develop. This creates a really exotic effect. Three of the best for this are *Paulownia tomentosa*, with big heart leaves (you can raise it from seed), *Ailanthus glandulosa*, the tree of heaven, with pinnate leaves and *Rhus glabra* 'Laciniata' (better than *R. typhina*), also pinnate, from a naturally suckering shrub. The last has bright autumn colour. Don't start hacking at these too hard until they've had a year or two to establish strongly. I should like to see the paulownia grouped with giant annual sunflowers (*Helianthus*).

CLIMBERS

Climbers have two particular values in a mixed border. They can prolong or add another dimension to a shrub's season by being allowed to grow through or over it; or they may be trained as vertical features on their own supports. Either way they take up little or no border space; no special sites have to be allowed for them and so, to the plantsman, they are a bonus that can be fitted in without thereby excluding something else.

You can train an ivy up a pole. Rising above a sea of lesser plants it will make a conspicuous and important feature. I have grown *Hedera canariensis* 'Variegata' on a chestnut pole for many years. Having quickly reached the top, its young shoots explored the air like feelers reaching towards outer space. Every year, I trim it hard back to the pole. This, at the end of the first 8 or 10 years, rotted, the weak spot being, as usual, at ground level. You cannot take ivy off a pole so I cut it down and put a new pole in (about 10 ft (3 m) long). The ivy didn't take long to cover its new support. This has never given way again and I suspect that the ivy now supports the pole.

Clematis make a good vertical feature on a pole, too. I find this a preferable support to a tripod. It takes up less room and the clematis hides it more efficiently. Clematis flowering from late June or early July onwards, on their young wood, are the most suitable. My most faithful example has been a C. × jackmanii 'Superba', planted 25 years ago. I cut it down to the ground every year, then tie in its young shoots with tarred string (soft string is tweaked off by sparrows for nesting material) as they rise. A step ladder is needed for the last ties. A column of purple blossom is the result and looks good behind a 6–7 ft (1.8–2.1 m) group of the yellow Senecio doria, which is rather like a giant ragwort but with plain, undivided leaves.

Clematis can be used throughout a mixed border to liven up the shrubs. Wherever you see a shrub looking a bit dull, ask yourself which clematis would look well growing with it. You must take care to match the vigour of one with the other so that the clematis does not overwhelm its host. If the weight and volume of a clematis seems to be too much for its supporter, you can knock a pole in and train some of the clematis up that, the rest over the shrub.

Climbing honeysuckles can be treated in the same way. I have Lonicera × americana on a pole devoted to it alone. On other occasions I find wild honeysuckle seeding into my borders and sometimes in a place where I can leave it; for instance, growing up Eucryphia 'Nymansay'. The honeysuckle growth has to be curbed every few years or it would strangle its host but it flowers earlier than the eucryphia and thus prolongs its season. Another good self-choice was over a clump of female skimmias. These look dull in June-July, when the honeysuckle is in bloom. Later, the berries of the one vie with the berries of the other, both in red clusters.

On a strong tree/shrub you can grow a Virginia creeper, Parthenocissus quinquifolia, or, less vigorous, P. henryana. But even better in some cases would be P. inserta, which is a tendril climber without adhesive discs (which are unnecessary in the circumstances). I grow this through the gaunt, double white lilac, Syringa 'Mme Lemoine'. So far the lilac, whose root system is terrific, has the upper hand. I should have planted the climber at some distance from the lilac's trunk and trained it into some outer branches up a strand of string. This policy also works well with clematis, when it is dark, dry and rooty close to its host's trunk.

39

The herbaceous perennial species of pea have a place in your border. Gertrude Jekyll used to train the white-flowered form of *Lathyrus latifolius* to cover up the withering remains of *Gypsophila paniculata* in late summer. The bricky red *L. rotundifolius* could be used likewise. *Lathyrus grandiflorus* is the everlasting pea, not everlasting *sweet* pea, as you so often hear; none of these perennial peas has any scent. It has sizeable magenta flowers and looks particularly well, I think, in a large specimen of purple leaved barberry (*Berberis × ottawensis* 'Purpurea', for instance) or a not so much pruned, purple *Cotinus coggygria*. But its tuberous root system is invasive and you may sometimes need to read the riot act. This may also be the case with the flame nasturtium, *Tropaeolum speciosum*, which you will consider a weed if you live in the northwest of Scotland but a cherished prize in southeast England. It can do well in the drier southeast if the soil is not alkaline. The flowers, throughout the summer and early autumn, are a very special shade of intense red. It looks particularly well over azaleas and other rhododendrons, out of their own season. The tuberous roots are great travellers and hard to catch, so this is a plant not freely available.

Nasturtiums are tropaeolums (*T. majus*) and they are to our purpose, although you must vigilantly prevent their self-sown seedlings from overpowering smaller plants. It looks marvellous to see trails of red nasturtiums flinging themselves over a mauve mound of *Aster sedifolius* (*A. acris*), for instance or into the cream plumes of *Artemisia lactiflora*. Or, for that matter, up the hedge that forms the background to your border. Nasturtiums do need a little attention, at times. They dislike drought and they are often attacked by black aphids and by cabbage white (the Large White) caterpillars.

ROSES

To treat roses separately is merely to acknowledge that they are a particularly important class of shrub. As all roses are shrubs, we are indulging in tautology when we speak of shrub roses. The roses we mean to include under this title are those that do not readily lend themselves to bedding. They do not conform to the herd instict but behave more as individuals. Often they are individually large plants, and there is then little incentive to grouping them.

As individuals, they are still most often lacking in style. The massive legs and hostile thorns are still in evidence. This is where their inclusion in a mixed border can have such an enormous advantage. If you grow blue and white *Campanula persicifolia* through the centre of a congenitally scrawny 'Crested Moss' rose, not only will they flower delightfully together but the rose's spindly legs will vanish from sight.

Bulbs will achieve the same object. For instance, underneath the skirts of a dwarfish rose 'The Fairy' suitable for a border's margin, you can grow the 15 in. (38 cm) tall Chinese chives, *Allium tuberosum*, which flowers in late summer. Its white, green-centred umbels will push through the rose and appear among the latter's pink blooms.

If the stiffness of a rose is on a large scale, as it would be in 'Queen Elizabeth' or 'Chinatown', grow a clematis like 'Perle d'Azur' through it. A large specimen of *Rosa moyesii* could take the weight of a *Clematis flammula*, and the frothy white blossom of the one would coincide with the ripening red hips of the other.

Many roses will have the advantage, in your border, of a double season of interest; either flowers followed by fruits as in *R. moyesii*, *R. setipoda* and the Rugosa roses, or two crops of flowers. 'Florence May Morse' is my favourite in that respect, as it is such an excellent clear shade of red, and this is a colour none too easy to find in shrubs and hardy perennials. Another favourite repeat bloomer with me is 'Perle d'Or', which has miniature tea rose flowers, apricot, shading to off-white at the margins, on a 5 ft (1.5 m) shrub. Its second crop tends to be particularly well scented on the air, thanks, most probably, to the moisture-laden air of early autumn.

Roses are not nearly so subject to their usual range of diseases – rust, black spot, mildew and the like – in a mixed community. But you will be queering your own pitch if you start massing roses in a mixed border. That would defeat the object of the exercise.

As with other shrubs, it will be wise to avoid most of those roses which contribute but the one flowering, in June, and have nothing further to offer, unless you are clever enough to substitute a climber going through them which will compensate with plenty of later blossom yet without destroying its host's sound health.

Hardy Perennials

Don't let the hardy plants be squeezed out by the shrubs. They are the great providers of splodges of bright colour (and I include white as such) in high summer. In this role there is nothing among the shrubs to touch them.

Before discussing some of the principals, let me say something about stature. In order to accommodate them to small gardens and also to cut out the effort of providing support, plant breeders have reduced the height of many plants which naturally grow quite tall. The trouble with these induced dwarfs is that most of them have a rather tight, bunched up appearance. Few inherit the grace of their tall antecedents. On the whole, then, I would say that where short plants are called for it is best (and quite simple) to use those that are naturally low growing, like *Crepis incana, Carlina acaulis, Epilobium glabellum, Sedum spectabile* (and most other sedums), violas, the lower cranesbills, diascias and hostas. And it would be my same recommendation for the annuals and bedding plants.

Of many campanulas for a mixed border, the queen, perhaps, is *Campanula lactiflora* but, at 7 ft (2.1 m) or so and requiring support, it can grow inordinately tall. The tiny 'Pouffe', on the other hand, is one of those induced dwarfs of which I have just been writing. The answer is 'Prichard's Variety'. This grows about 3 ft (90 cm) tall and is a darker, more definite shade of campanula blue than some of the rather milky mauves.

There is nothing to touch delphiniums, but they do leave rather a gap. Treating them as short-lived perennials to be renewed fairly frequently from seed, you can afford to cut them right down after flowering (a slightly weakening operation) and wait for new growth to give you a second crop of flowers in September. Secondary growth in delphiniums will always be attacked by mildew but you can anticipate by watering your plants with Benlate (benomyl) when the young shoots appear. New delphinium seed strains are constantly appearing. I have had good results with 'Blue Fountain', said to be a mere 2¼ ft (70 cm) tall, but in their second year, at any rate, they will run up to 5 ft (1.5 m) or more. I don't like them too short anyway.

Lupins are a nuisance in most mixed borders because they flower early and look a wreck, however you treat them, from mid or late June onwards. If you must grow them (and I certainly must),

42

treat them as biennials. Raise a new batch from seed each spring, grow them on in a spare plot till autumn planting out time. Then, throw them out at midsummer and replace with an annual raised from seed sown in May. (See illustrations pp. 12–13).

Oriental poppies (from *Papaver orientale* and its relatives) provide a marvellous foretaste of summer and can be included in a July border without weakening the main impact. They do not resent being cut to the ground after flowering, which enables you to plant very close to their roots with bedding plants such as dahlias or cannas. The most upstanding poppy, generally requiring no support, is *P. bracteatum* 'Goliath', which grows 4 ft (1.2 m) tall and carries enormous blood red blooms of the greatest delicacy in texture.

I nowadays exclude peonies (*Paeonia lactiflora* and *P. officinalis* cultivars) from my borders, because their season is so short and they become passengers from late June which you cannot readily mask. However, you could try growing a plant of *Lathyrus latifolius* (see p. 40) or of *Clematis flammula* (with masses of scented white blossom in August-September) behind a peony group and allow the climber to take over in the latter part of the season. Otherwise I recommend growing peonies in a picking plot.

Of the michaelmas daisy tribe, most have too late and short a season to be useful. Such are the cultivars of *Aster novae-angliae* and *A. novi-belgii*. By far the most rewarding is the lavender coloured *A. × frikartii* 'Moench', which starts flowering in early August and carries on for two months. Growing $2\frac{1}{2}$–3 ft (75–90 cm) tall, it is self-supporting after the first year and its flowers are quite large as asters go. I like it with a yellow *Heliopsis* (one of the perennial sunflowers) such as 'Golden Plume' $3\frac{1}{2}$ ft (1 m).

Shasta daisies, *Chrysanthemum maximum*, tend to be a somewhat baleful and corpse-like white, with heavy green foliage that doesn't help any. The single-flowered kinds have the great merit of a yellow central disc, which gives colour relief. My own favourite is 'Everest' 4 ft (1.2 m) which has the largest single flowers, especially if you replant with small pieces every other year. Size does not lead to grossness, here.

Border phloxes – *Phlox paniculata* and *P. maculata* cultivars – are a marvellous standby in July and August on heavy, moisture-retaining soils. Healthy stock, free of eelworm (nematode) infection is paramount. For this reason I seldom buy a plant from a nursery, preferring to beg a piece from a friend's garden in which I can see that the plants have nothing wrong with them. When infected by eelworm, the leaves of phlox become puckered and many of them drawn out to fine threads. Once seen, never forgotten. Don't bother about the names of phloxes. Be guided by

43

the colours you like and the robustness with which they grow. Phloxes are greedy and thirsty. They need replanting in improved soil every fourth year. If you try switching positions with them you'll find they get all mixed up, as pieces of root left behind make new plants.

The most effective *Monarda*, the bee balm, smelling of lemons, is 'Cambridge Scarlet', which is really a good crimson red and not scarlet. It flowers in July and there's nothing to compare with a healthy quilt of it then. Subject to mildew, however, and to dying out in winter. 'Cobham Beauty' is nice, with pink flowers and purple bracts. A top dressing with old potting soil, when the young shoots are 2 in. (5 cm) high in spring, helps to prevent the colony from starving itself out.

The yellow-flowered yarrows have a strong personality in a border, especially *Achillea filipendulina* 'Gold Plate', 5 ft (1.5 m), and 'Coronation Gold', 3 ft (90 cm). They carry table-top corymbs of mustard yellow flowers in July, gradually losing freshness just as made up English mustard does when it is kept too long. Use with restraint. At 2½ ft (75 cm) A. 'Moonshine' is a paler but still bright yellow, set off by silvery foliage. Old colonies tend to stop flowering and become foliage plants only. Prettiest of the lot is the pale lemon yellow, 2 ft (60 cm) *A.* × *taygetea*, but it is less robust than the others and not always winter hardy; it is worth a bit of trouble, however. The white forms of *A. ptarmica* are of secondary value, except for cutting. Their running habit with slender white rhizomes is a great nuisance.

Opposite: *Viola cornuta* 'Alba', *Rosa pimpinellifolia* 'William III', *Hosta sieboldiana* 'Elegans' and *Alchemilla mollis*
Above: Foliage contrast with hosta and climbing golden hop (supported)
Below: Suitable for shade – hosta and fern with double pink campion (*Melandrium rubrum* 'Flore Pleno')

Except in rather moist woodland settings, I have gone off the majority of astilbes, as they flower for too short a time (a fortnight). True the inflorescence never looks ugly after flowering but they are among the first plants to look unhappy when water is short. Exceptionally, the 3½ ft (1 m) Astilbe taquetii has a long season, starting rather late; beautiful foliage, rather narrow panicles of a singularly bright mauve. Lovely contrasted with the heads of pink hortensia hydrangeas. It seeds itself in a most agreeable manner so that you find outliers from your main colony.

Hemerocallis, the day lilies, have attained enormous popularity and you need to be careful in your selection. Visit the RHS trial at Wisley in July. Some with beautiful blooms are not sufficiently free with them at any one time. It is also a good idea to stand back from a clump and see how well it shows up in the distance. Many day lily colours are too lurid or muddy to be seen except at close quarters. Remember that the plant itself is far from neat. 'Corky' (yellow) and 'Golden Chimes' (bronze and yellow) are exceptionally prolific though individual flowers are small. These are only 2½ ft (75 cm) tall. So is H. flava, the earliest to flower (early June) and the sweetest scented. This is clear yellow, but the earliness of its season is a disadvantage. If you get bored with its foliage, cut it right down after flowering. It will soon grow again and remain fresh until autumn 'Marion Vaughn' is a luminous, large flowered pale yellow for late July and August. Hemerocallis lend themselves to interplanting with narcissi and jonquils.

The hostas are even more popular than the day lilies. Although particularly suited to shade, they will often put up a remarkable performance when hot and dry. In the main they must be considered as foliage plants, particularly suited to shrubbery margins in the early part of their season. For later effect, Hosta ventricosa 'Variegata' ('Aureo-Marginata' in the States) not only retains a lively creamy yellow margin to its broad heart leaves but flowers abundantly, to great effect with spires of lavender bells. That is in July, which is also the flowering season of H. lancifolia (running through August) with flared trumpet flowers at 15 in. (38 cm) and 'Tall Boy', with similar flowers but upstanding to 4–5 ft (1.2–1.5 m).

A healthy colony of H. crispula (all hostas are subject to virus disease) looks even smarter, with its broad white leaf margin, than the more robust and frequently seen 'Thomas Hogg'. Both need shade to protect the white from sun scorch. They show up well beneath a Fatsia japonica whose lower branches have been removed. Here also you could grow ferns for leaf contrast and interplant with snowdrops for early interest. This is the essence of mixed border gardening. Another hosta for this setting would be H. undulata, of petite habit and variegated in streaks throughout the leaves which have an elegant twist on them.

The glaucous-leaved hostas need more sun to bring out their blue colouring. H. sieboldiana 'Elegans' is one of the best known and largest-leaved with a rippling texture. Some of the modern hybrids (like 'Buckshaw Blue') are so blue as scarcely to look real. They are pristine in spring and early summer and tend to look tired from July onwards. Hosta plantaginea is then at its best, however, its yellow-green foliage retaining a remarkable freshness until September. The pick of the hybrids from this is 'Royal Standard' (far better than 'Honey Bells') with night-scented white trumpets in late summer.

Blue-leaved hostas look uncommonly well close to another genus of moisture-loving foliage plants, Rodgersia. The most striking is R. pinnata 'Superba', whose bold, pinnate leaves are purple in May. It flowers freely and the inflorescence is a pink panicle, in late June, gradually darkening as it ages to dusky red in autumn. Thus its season of beauty is five months long. Rodgersia podophylla has leaflets like a webbed foot. They take on rosy autumnal colouring from midsummer onwards but can scorch under stress.

Sedums, by contrast, are great drought resisters. 'Autumn Joy' is a mainstay in every garden. You do not want to be overloaded with it in a summer border, but even then its green broccoli-like heads of buds make a distinct impression. The flowers are pale dusky pink in late August, gradually deepening to a warm autumnal red; finally brown and holding their shape throughout the winter. Sedum spectabile is the one that butterflies go for in a big way and it is pure pink, more intense in 'Brilliant'. This is only 1 ft (30 cm) tall, against 'Autumn Joy's' 18 in. (45 cm). S. spectabile flowers in August with a moderately brief season. Sedum maximum 'Atropurpureum' is a rather coarse 2 ft (60 cm) plant with deep purple leaves, for which it is grown, and dusky flowers. Not an easy plant to place effectively, it is shown up well when inter-planted with the grey foliage of Senecio cineraria (see p. 35).

Sedum 'Ruby Glow' is nearly prostrate and can be overplanted with bulbs. Allium christophii is a suitable choice as its big globes, in flower in June, continue to look handsome when dying, at which time, in August-September, the sedum is in its stride, with purplish red flowers. 'Vera Jameson' is another purple-leaved sedum neater than the others, about 1 ft (30 cm) tall.

The vast genus Salvia (the sages) includes tender and hardy plants, shrubs, annuals and biennials. S. guaranitica starts flower-ing in August and is deep blue, contrasting well with yellow or with the orange of Tithonia rotundifolia 'Torch' (an annual). The sage grows 3 ft (90 cm) tall and is tuberous rooted, not reliably hardy. Lift at least one root each autumn to overwinter under glass. Easily raised from spring cuttings from young shoots. It is safest to

overwinter a clump of *Salvia uliginosa* in the same way. It makes a forest of 5 ft (1.5 m) shoots bearing short spikes of clear, rather light blue flowers. Not a common colour in its August season.

Salvia nemorosa 'Superba' is the pick of the hardy perennials, a fairly massive plant to $3\frac{1}{2}$ ft (1 m) (safer with some support) and carrying a mass of blue purple flower spikes in which the bracts are reddish purple. A lovely contrast to the scarlet domes of *Lychnis chalcedonica* (but see p. 16) in July. There are some good dwarf earlier flowering kinds (with more being developed in Germany) but they do not have the staying power of 'Superba' with its capacity for producing a second crop in September. 'East Friesland' is a fine purple dwarf, at 18 in. (45 cm), and makes a delightful partner for the flat heads of the pale yellow *Achillea × taygetea*.

In the mixed border context, *Lychnis coronaria* should not be omitted. It has grey, felted leaves and stems which highlight its brilliant magenta disc flowers from early July to late August. These harmonise well with the dusky pink and grey-green tones of *Fuchsia magellanica* 'Versicolor', while the biennial or at least mono-carpic *Eryngium giganteum*, a 3 ft (90 cm) sea holly with ghost pale bracts and sea green flowers, would make up an excellent trio. The eryngium self-sows and the lychnis must be depended upon to do the same, as it exhausts itself after two years' flowering. So your colonies of each will continually be jostling for supremacy.

Opposite: Globe flower (*Trollius* 'Canary Bird') and *Ranunculus aconitifolius* 'Flore Pleno', overhung in shady border by *Hydrangea* 'Quadricolor'. Above: Accent on yellow, with kniphofia backed by golden-variegated dogwood. Below: Yellow and white border, with Spanish broom, rose 'Iceberg' and *Oenothera missouriensis* in foreground

I have not yet mentioned *Iris* and, indeed, the bearded kinds are not at all good as mixed border plants. It isn't simply because they flower too early and for too short a season but because their leaves look tired and usually spotted from late June onwards and there is no way of masking or interplanting them. They need to have the sun beating on their rhizomes. In a large border you can accommodate a few of the *I. sibirica* and *I. spuria* types and hope that they will not be too noticeable after their faded flower heads have been removed.

Neither have I found perennial *Dianthus* to be very satisfactory mixed border plants. Those with a long flowering season make the least comely plants. They have to be grown at the border's margin and there is no hope of disguising their shortcomings here. Pinks are happiest in dry walls or paving or in hot raised borders.

Geraniums, the hardy cranesbills, include a great many suitable members. Many are good in shade, so that they will flourish among and under the branches of shrubs. Such is the bright mauve-pink *Geranium endressii*, with a long season from May onwards. 'Wargrave' is a salmon pink cultivar and 'A.T. Johnson' a clearer, paler chalky pink but this last can be excessively vigorous, killing out its neighbours. A hard cut-back in mid-season is often a good plan. *Geranium psilostemon* often needs support at $3\frac{1}{2}$ ft (1 m) but its intense magenta with a near black eye is most arresting. More valuable still, in the future, when a way of propagating it quickly and in quantity has been found, will be 'Ann Folkard', which has the same colouring but is a bushy plant no more than 2 ft (60 cm) tall and with a far more extended flowering season. There are a number of selected forms in meadow cranesbill, *G. pratense*, including a double 'blue' and a double purple ('Plenum Caeruleum' and 'Plenum Violaceum'). They all need support.

The magenta-flowered bloody cranesbill, *G. sanguineum*, is excellent at a border's margin. I have it in front of a pale grey *Santolina pinnata neapolitana* (see p. 35). There is a brilliant pink variant called 'Shepherd's Warning'. But the most rewarding marginal cranesbill of all, making a huge pool of magenta that spreads forwards and filters up into any thing a little taller than itself, is 'Russell Prichard'. It flowers from May to November and does not even require a mid-season trimming.

Geranium wallichianum 'Buxton's Blue' is very special, late in the season. It makes a rambling mat that reaches wide but dies right back to its crown in the winter. As it gets going late in spring, you can surround it with small bulbs like alliums (I have the pink, May-flowering *Allium murrayanum*), crocuses, scillas and chionodoxas. 'Buxton's Blue' starts flowering in July but its colour tends to be a slightly muddy mauve in hot weather. Later it becomes blue with a white centre and purple stamens, continuing into late October.

Mass rather than structure is by no means an invariable attribute in herbaceous perennials. Some make an exceedingly bold impact and will stand out, structurally, when seen right across a garden. They are often referred to as architectural plants.

Such is *Veratrum album*, a member of the lily family with pleated foliage not unlike a hosta's or a giant plantain's. The 5 ft (1.5 m) inflorescence is composed of many white stars which are set along a branching panicle. It is extremely hardy, but uncommon because slow to propagate (from seed). Even if a nurseryman has the patience to bring a plant on to flowering size in five years or so, he is unlikely to command the price he deserves. Gardeners in Britain are extraordinarily mean about paying a realistic price for a hardy plant although they'll dig into their purses for a choice rhododendron without a murmur.

Acanthus are almost too easily propagated, from every piece of root, but they still need quite a bit of managing when being raised for sale. Their long, purplish spikes of hooded flowers have a sinister magnetism. *Acanthus balcanicus* (generally listed as *A. longifolius*), is one of the freest flowering and only 3 ft (90 cm) tall. *Acanthus spinosus* is taller and has handsomer leaves, while *A. mollis* has splendid soapy-textured foliage but is apt to be shy flowering.

The most desirable perennial eryngiums are often in short supply. Specially arresting is *E. × oliverianum*, 3 ft (90 cm) tall (rather floppy from the base) with steely blue stems and fairly large blue flower heads and bracts. Quite different, but a splendid mixed border ingredient if it will survive your winters (and it is not so very tender) is the Uraguayan species *E. decaisneanum* (*E. pandanifolium*). It has long, sea green, scimitar leaves. They are evergreen and spiny on the margins (don't poke your eye with them). The branching inflorescence is modest in colouring but rises to 8 ft (2.4 m) in autumn and has an imposing presence.

Kniphofias, the red hot pokers, always stand out when in flower, though their season is often on the short side. *Cynara cardunculus*, the cardoon, has magnificent glaucous cut leaves followed by magnificent blue thistle heads – very close to the globe artichoke but more numerous, spinier, and up to 7–8 ft (2.1–2.4 m).

A plant does not have to be tall to be impressive, so long as its inflorescence has good bones. Such is *Carlina acaulis*, a 1 ft (30 cm) tall thistle with wide, bleached heads surrounded by a ruff of leaf-like bracts. In damp weather it remains doggedly closed, but when expanded in sunshine it is besieged by bees and butterflies.

51

Above: Tender bedding with perennial alstroemerias and shrubby potentilla in Cottage Garden, Sissinghurst Castle
Below: Late September free-for-all with annual *Linum grandiflorum* 'Rubrum' dominant

Above: Tulip 'Orange Favourite' and self-sowing biennial white honesty give early interest
Below: July mixture, including yellow *Asphodeline liburnica* which opens late afternoon

Ornamental Grasses and Bamboos

In gardening terms, grasses are either clump formers or else they are spreaders and colonisers. Whatever their habit, but especially if they are colonisers, these grasses, however ornamental in themselves, look a mess when you pen them into a bed of their own. Their long narrow leaves need contrasts. Nothing easier than to give it them in a mixed border context. They contrast particularly well with dwarf conifers, especially those that flower above their evergreen partners. In my mixed border I have recently planted a *Pinus mugo* in front of the tall *Miscanthus sinensis* 'Silver Feather'. With such a length of leaf and stalk before you reach its flowers, at the 7 ft (2.1 m) level, the grass needs something blocky by its side. I had thought of *Pittosporum tobira*, but that would not have been hardy enough, as I discovered when I lost it the previous winter! *Euphorbia wulfenii* would do the trick or *Daphne pontica*, if it didn't have to pant too much in the sun.

Miscanthus floridulus is another stately grass whose appearance becomes unnecessarily stemmy in its nether regions in the latter part of its growing season unless some sort of 3 ft (90 cm) plant can fill in there. This grass grows to 9 ft (2.7 m) or more (far less in the cooler north) between spring and autumn and, with its outward-curving leaves, looks like a foliar fountain. On a perfectly still summer's evening it could be wrought in metal, but usually it converses with a companionable rustle.

I emphasised, earlier, the importance of making plant groups in a border, so as to avoid the fidgets, but the taller, clump-forming grasses are something of an exception. Single clumps among lower neighbours can make a powerful impression. And there is a symmetry about a solo plant which may be lost when several are grown close together so that they interfere with one another at their points of contact. In a very large planting scheme such as you would expect in a public garden, grouping becomes necessary, but in our own private gardens, even when of quite a size, seldom.

And so, if your border has considerable depth, bring your grasses to or near the margin or to a corner or promontory. Don't be inhibited by the old rule, tallest at the back, shortest at the front. That, once learned, should be freely broken. The tall parts of grasses are, most usually, the inflorescences and they tend to be of diaphanous texture. You can see through them to lower plants beyond. To take some examples:

The tallest we can grow is the giant reed grass, Arundo donax. In a warm summer it will soar to 15 ft (4.5 m) but it is still self supporting. Its leaves are broadish and a beautiful shade of blue. At Wisley (appropriate to mention in a Wisley Handbook), it is grown at the back of the double borders (mixed but not wholeheartedly mixed) on the way up to Battleston Hill. With a tall beech hedge immediately behind them, they make scarcely any impression. If brought halfway to the front they would stand forth as they should. In an island bed, however, this grass could be near the centre and make its presence quite sufficiently felt. I have recently planted one in the midst of a largish colony of hydrangeas and there is another, already established, near to their margin.

I have already mentioned Miscanthus floridulus. Of M. sinensis 'Silver Feather' it should additionally be said that it is, to date (but this will change), the one clone within this genus so far grown in this country that can be relied upon to flower well before the autumn. The others can and should still be grown as foliage plants but they cannot be relied upon to flower properly before the end of their growing season. Not in this country. Miscanthus sinensis 'Gracillimus' has very narrow leaves with a pale median stripe. It grows about 5 ft (1.5 m) tall and dies off warm russet, so that it continues to look beautiful into the New Year.

There are two zebra grasses, both of this species and seldom distinguished in the trade which lumps them both under 'Zebrinus'. Their leaves in both cases are interrupted across a green blade by patches of yellow, faint early in the season but becoming increasingly distinct, especially in a sunny position. The habit of 'Zebrinus' is loose, with arching foliage, whereas in 'Strictus' growth is stiffer, the leaves pointing obliquely upwards. Both are good. 'Strictus' is the hardier. 'Variegatus', 4 ft (1.2 m), is extremely pretty, being variegated longitudinally with pale cream marginal stripes. It makes an excellent solo specimen but I do think it contrasts marvellously with the broad foliage of a purple-leaved canna like 'Wyoming' or Canna indica 'Purpurea'. They are both approximately the same height and so, rather than plant them side by side, I would allow a gap in which a patch of some quite low-growing plant could link them. It could be the grey shrub Helichrysum splendidum (see p. 35), or perhaps a patch of white-flowered busy lizzies, e.g. Impatiens 'Futura White', an F_1 strain.

Stipa gigantea loves a light soil, sand or chalk. Clumps that begin to die out in patches should be replanted in late spring. Never disturb your grasses in autumn unless they belong to some other member of the household whom you wish to kill by proxy. This is another clumpy grass, its low foliage totally undistinguished, but its flowering stems run up to 6 ft (1.8 m) and they resemble an oat but

Above: A fountain of *Miscanthus sinensis* 'Variegatus' with *Spiraea* 'Goldflame', 30 June
Below: Important grass features, *Calamagrostis* × *acutiflora* 'Stricta' with pampas *Cortaderia selloana* 'Pumila' on either side, 21 October

with much wider sprays and each unit therein distinct so that they make a diaphanous, rose-tinted gauze, marvellous seen against low sunlight. That is at midsummer but the display lasts as the flowers bleach with age. Get this on or near a promontory or corner.

So also *Molina caerulea altissima* 'Windspiel', which again has long, flowering stems above low groundwork. It may be outside your border's main season as it flowers in autumn, as does *M.*

Above: Liriope muscari and *Colchicum* 'The Giant', 9 September
Below: Beth Chatto Water Garden, with *Eupatorium purpureum*, two
miscanthus, *Gunnera chilensis*, 31 August

caerulea 'Variegata'. This, however, has interesting greenish-yellow-variegated foliage but the haze of purple flowers is charming. They are only 2 ft (60 cm) tall. It is still an excellent corner or promontory plant and you can group it but allow 18 ins. (45 cm) between clumps so that they do not interfere one with another.

For grass fans, I strongly recommend *Calamagrostis × acutiflora* 'Stricta', to make an upstanding 6 ft (1.8 m) feature among lower flowers or foliage. I have ferns around mine but they are in full sunshine, as the grass should be. It makes a forest of dead-straight flowering stems to its full height and the inflorescence.is soft mole and grey squirrel at first, bleaching as it dies to straw and remaining an asset for quite five months.

Pampas grass is not necessarily easy to accommodate in a mixed border because its saw-edged leaves spread outwards and are unkind to its neighbours. Best, given fairly dense plantings, is *Cortaderia sellgana* 'Pumila', whose leaves are reasonably short. Its upright brushes are cream, with a sheen on them when young and they develop (to 5 ft (1.5 m)) in late September, so this would be an unacceptable passenger in a July-August border.

Most of the grasses I have described are pretty tall, but if not of spreading habit, this need not deter the owners of small gardens. A grass for them, however, is *Hakonechloa macra* 'Aureola'. It is only 12 in. (30 cm) tall and its abundance of yellow, green-striped leaves arch outwards leaving the centre open like the crown of a Shidsu dog's head. This is a plant that takes time to establish but does not then need disturbing.

Carex stricta 'Bowles's Golden', *Glyceria maxima* 'Variegata' and *Phalaris arundinacea* 'Picta' have it in common that they will grow under water but, equally, can be used as border plants. In which position the last two are rather similar, with green and white variegation and a running rootstock. *Glyceria* is the more invasive but can be treated as a bedding plant. *Phalaris*, called gardener's garters or ribbon grass, becomes tired looking when it has run up to flower in July. I like to cut it all to the ground and let it sprout again. The carex, a sedge, makes clumps of golden-variegated leaves that are brightest in early summer but last well and harmonise with orange and yellow flowers, while providing a contrast of form.

Pennisetum are grown for their flowers which are soft and fluffy like a woolly bear caterpillar. *Pennisetum orientale*, although only 15 in. (38 cm) high, makes a mound of blossom rose tinted at first becoming grey, which still looks best if not closed in by tall neighbours. Charming with the pink dandelion flowers of *Crepis incana*. *Pennisetum villosum* can be and usually is treated as an annual. It is prolific in its flowers which, at Sissinghurst Castle, are specially effective at the border's front with *Sedum* 'Autumn Joy' and the grey, pinnate foliage of *Senecio leucostachys*, which is a tender shrub. I had always wondered what to plant with *Ophiopogon planiscapus* 'Nigrescens', so as to pep up and show off its ultra dark, purple-black strap leaves, which never rise far off the ground. In the USA I saw the answer. It was interplanted with a foot-tall, prick-eared grass, *Imperata cylindrica* 'Rubra', in which the reddish blades are constantly shot through with sunlight so that they glow like rubies, but especially late and early in the day. This again would make a good planting on a border's promontory, although a small border where nothing was very high or any marginal position would serve.

Bamboos do not die back in the winter. They are shrubby grasses. Some, with a furiously running rootstock, are quite unfit for polite society. That is to say they will not mix with anything although in themselves they may, like the sasas, be quite beautiful. Others may be clump-forming as a rule and these make good mixers. But you can never be quite sure, even then. A bamboo that is generally clump-forming may, if it finds itself in rich moist soil and the weather unusually warm, suddenly behave quite differently. I would normally, in Britain, recommend the genus *Phyllostachys* as being among the most handsome and reliably behaving of bamboos. But I have recently seen how it can go berserk where the summers are warm (this was in North Carolina). Perhaps even in south Devon I might be surprised at its performance compared with east Sussex.

Anyway, assuming that *Phyllostachys* are for you and that, should they wander a little, you will have no difficulty in chopping out the errant pieces, *P. nigra* in its several varieties is strongly to be recommended. It grows to about 10 ft (3 m) and presents itself stylishly. *Phyllostachys viridiglaucescens* is a good do-er to cut your teeth on and see whether these bamboos are for you. It grows to 15 ft (4.5 m) (depending, again, on your climate) and is of pleasingly cheerful yellow-green colouring. It increases in girth faster than most. *Phyllostachys bambusoides* and *P. flexuosa* are unsuitable in a mixed border because their canes splay outwards and get in the way of neighbouring plants.

Of the tall, hardy *Arundinaria*, *A. murielae* has a better, more up-standing habit (to 8–10 ft (2.4–3 m)) than the over-flexible *A. nitida*. Also it remains more compact, but will make a very large clump in time and may need reducing at the margins. It has the advantage (sometimes) of availability. Nurserymen in this country are making only the feeblest efforts to supply stocks of *Phyllostachys*.

Bamboos do repay a little looking after, by cutting out, each spring, dead or tired old canes. A thinned out clump looks as smart as a thick-coated dog after being stripped.

A stylish dwarf bamboo, only 2–2½ ft (60–75 cm) tall, of strong appearance and with little propensity to running is Shibatea kumasasa. It does like plenty of moisture.

A much more slender-caned but only slightly running bamboo and then only if it really likes you, is Arundinaria viridistriata (A. auricoma), whose leaves are striped in yellow and green. It looks much its brightest and freshest if cut to the ground every year, in April, and it will then grow no more than 2 ft (60 cm) high. For the border margin, then. I have it next to the glaucous foliage (and white flowers) of seakale, Crambe maritima, while behind it is a dark, solid block of Mahonia 'Undulata', with wavy-margined and exceptionally shiny evergreen foliage.

Another good low one is A. variegata, with lively green and white variegation. It could grow more than 3 ft (90 cm) tall, if allowed to, but I keep it to 2 ft (60 cm) by cutting it back every second or third year. When established, this can run quite a bit, but very charmingly. The insidious nature of the beast is to send a long, branching rhizome horizontally underground to a distance of 3–4 ft (90 cm–1.2 m) from the main colony, and it may go through the roots of a shrub, like a rose, which is awkward. Especially as you see no sign of what is happening until the next year, when the first above-ground shoots are made. A bit of exploratory digging round your official clump each winter is to be recommended.

There are two excellent plants, sometimes mistaken for bamboos, that are worth bringing in at this point. Danaë racemosa is actually related to asparagus (I am often tempted to eat its young shoots). Its branching stems are luxuriantly clothed in pointed, glossy green foliage, which is evergreen, but each stem lives only for a couple of years and so you must help the plant to rejuvenate itself. Stems that you cut out, in spring, may still be quite fresh and look well arranged with daffodils. In fact I grow the early 'February Gold' among my danaë, which are only a little taller themselves. This plant is highly shade tolerant. Sometimes it produces the odd bright orange berry and you wish it would do more.

Nandina domestica is a shrub to 3–4 ft (90 cm–1.2 m) with large leaves that are finely divided into elegant lanceolate leaflets, coppery when young. The white flower trusses are unimportant but a bonus. In warmer climates they are followed by spectacular crops of red berries. Better not to think about them.

Ferns

Ferns are particularly appropriate for growing among and underneath shrubs, whether deciduous or evergreen. You tolerate a shrub for so long, clothed with branches to ground level. Then, as its bulk increases, you think 'this is getting too much' and you remove its lowest branches so that it becomes a tree in miniature, albeit a many-stemmed tree. Now you can plant again, right into its centre.

An *Olearia macrodonta* will serve as an example. It is one of the New Zealand daisy bushes with evergrey-green holly-like leaves, with mock prickles and masses of clustered white flowers in June. Mine grew, from a baby out of a 5 in. (12 cm) pot, far bigger than I ever anticipated and would, if permitted, have engulfed a path on one side and a strip of lawn on the other. Between is the border in which it grew. So I made a 'tree' of it, as I have described, some 9 ft (2.7 m) high and far more across. It had beautiful peeling trunks. Underneath I grew the spring-flowering perennial, *Omphalodes cappadocica*, that resembles a large forget-me-not; an anemone, *Anemone hortensis*, with purple flowers in spring; the late flowering cranesbill, *Geranium wallichianum* 'Buxton's Blue'; *Campanula persicifolia*, which seeded itself where it wanted to be and poked out of the olearia's sides; finally, on either side of the bush, a rather precious evergreen fern, *Polystichum setiferum* 'Pulcherrimum Bevis', which is a mutant of the soft shield fern. All these are shade lovers, so I was thrown, somewhat, when the olearia (over a period of two years) died. Shrubby members of the Compositae are rather apt to do this, I find.

So, from being shade lovers my underplantings had to become sun baskers and they took this change of role absolutely in their stride.

In another instance I had *Blechnum chilense*, which is a carpeting, colonising fern, underneath a tree peony, *Paeonia delavayi*. That died of peony botrytis but the fern looks even better in the sun. Although its fronds are shorter, they grow more densely and their colouring from youth to maturity (new fronds appearing all through the summer) is much more varied in sun, starting coppery and maturing deep green.

I am not trying to suggest that all ferns are as happy in the sun as the shade. Some do scorch badly in a blazing position; the shuttlecock fern, *Matteuccia struthiopteris*, for instance. My point is that it is generally very useful to be able to grow ferns in shade but

61

it may, at times, also be useful to grow them in sun and it should not be assumed that this is stupid.

As with the grasses, you can, culturally, divide ferns into clump formers and colonisers. Polystichums are among the best of the clump formers. A great many variations on the theme have turned up over the years. Within *P. setiferum* these have been subdivided into the Acutilobum and the Divisilobum groups. The first have narrow, sharply pointed pinnules (the smallest subdivision of a frond), leaving spaces between, as in a grill or lattice screen. They are quite strong growers and clumps should never be planted so closely that the fronds of one grow into the fronds of another. This simply looks confused. Leave at least 3 ft (90 cm) between them and interplant with early bulbs. The old fronds should anyhow be cut away (generally in March but it can, for the sake of your bulb display, be done in the New Year) before the new ones unfurl, otherwise it is difficult to do the job without damaging the new in removing the old. If you don't do it at all, the ruff of old fronds will, as spring progresses, increasingly take from the beauty of the new.

That goes for any evergreen fern, such as *Blechnum*, *Polypodium*, *Asplenium scolopendrium* (the hartstongue) and other polystichums.

The Divisilobum group of *Polystichum setiferum* includes the Plumosum (feathery) types and all are soft, even mossy-textured.

Hartstongue ferns have a special value in their perfectly plain strap leaves, which can be contrasted with the more typically divided frond. In general, ferns of different kinds look better when not grown together, which leads to a certain monotony that confuses the eye, but in conjunction with quite different plants. Hosta leaves would generally make a striking contrast but ferns have such a presence of their own that you would do better to grow quite dwarf hostas among or close to them, rather than the dominant kinds which would compete at the ferns' own level.

Small things like celandines (*Ranunculus ficaria*), hepaticas, *Hacquetia epipactis* (with tiny yellow flowers surrounded by a green ruff), primroses and anemones make ideal companions. Later in the season, blocks of a colonising fern like *Polypodium vulgare* 'Cornubiense' look good alternating with fairly low growing hardy fuchsias, as it might be 'Tom Thumb' or 'Lady Thumb', 'Alice Hofman' or 'Poppet'. Hardy cyclamen, especially *Cyclamen hederifolium*, go well with dwarf ferns like *Blechnum penna-marina*.

You will often find that a wild fern, usually *Dryopteris filix-mas*, the male fern, has sown itself at the base of a shrub in your border. Take the hint. If it puts itself there it is a place where a more interesting fern will flourish. You can make the exchange.

Bulbs

Auxiliaries rather than protagonists is my attitude to bulbs in a mixed border, although there are exceptions. They lengthen the season at both ends without being allowed to detract from the main display, which I shall continue to assume to be in the height of summer.

You could regard them as an extension of your bedding out activities, in which case the spring flowerers would need to be removed at the end of May and replaced with annuals and summer bedding. I prefer to regard bulbs as permanencies in the mixed border. They should be sited where they seldom need to be disturbed, among perennials or underneath the skirts of shrubs. Since bulbs are out of sight for much of the year, it is wise to mark their positions, as you plant them, with short pieces of cane. Then, when next you're working in that area, the canes will remind you that there is something underneath. You could use a label, but nowadays I prefer to rely upon a note at the time of planting in my garden book.

The earliest bulbs go well beneath or among deciduous shrubs, completing their growth before the shrubs are casting much shade. Snowdrops (*Galanthus*) build into fat clumps and seed themselves freely, even under a rooty old lilac. A crocus like *Crocus tommasinianus* will seed itself so generously that you will find yourself digging up its corms in the dead season. Not to worry, just push the exposed corms back into the ground with the tip of your finger. Among a strong but spreading grower like *Geranium endressii* or *G. sanguineum*, *C. tommasinianus* can seed and cohabit without doing any harm. Its leaves are narrow enough not to look too bad for too long as they die off.

Scillas flower in March and are happy spreaders. I have planted a rich blue *Scilla bifolia* with the hardy perennial *Valeriana phu* 'Aurea', whose leaves are bright lime green, almost yellow, early in the season. *Scilla sibirica* is the brightest and best known species ('Spring Beauty' is indistinguishable from it) and colonises well among fuchsias, ceratostigmas, *Potentilla fruticosa*, perovskias and suchlike late developing shrubs that can be cut back in late winter or spring. I saw an interesting mixed planting that covered a long season at Brookside Gardens in Maryland. Overhead were purple-leaved *Prunus cerasifera* cut hard back annually for maximum foliage impact on a large shrub rather than a tree.

Opposite: The feathery yellow leaves of *Robinia pseudoacacia* 'Frisia' provide a bright splash of colour above hostas, brunneras, variegated weigela and other plants
Above: *Ceanothus × delileanus* 'Gloire de Versailles', *Rosa* 'Ethel' and the yellow day lily *Hemerocallis* 'Esther Walker'

Underneath was continuous cover at the foot-tall level of *Ceratostigma plumbaginoides*. This has deep blue, plumbago-type flowers in late summer and autumn and the leaves colour up well. It is a ground cover plant that gradually increases its range by suckering. With and underneath this (and the ceratostigma can all be cut away in winter) is a mass planting of tiny bulbs like scillas and chionodoxas, crocus and erythroniums – anything of low stature except for the grape hyacinth, *Muscari armenaicum*, whose lank foliage has a disagreeable habit of appearing in the autumn.

If you include *Narcissus*, restrict yourself to those kinds, mostly dwarfs, whose leaves are slender and will not, in May, make your border look as though it had finished for the year, when it has not even begun. Such is the 10 in. (25 cm) tall 'Hawera', a *N. triandrus* hybrid, neat, multiflowered, pale yellow. A very late flowerer like the yellow, jonquil-style 'Tittle Tattle', mixes well in a group of day lilies, because by the time its own foliage is looking ratty, the hemerocallis will have grown up enough to conceal the defect.

The May-flowering tulips are especially suitable, for the same reason, that their foliage is already engulfed among their perennial neighbours by the time it is yellowing. It helps matters to remove the flowered stems. You can plant them among Japanese anemones, *Rudbeckia* 'Goldsturm' (a late starting black-eyed Susan, flowering from August on), lupins. Also at the front of threadbare shrubs like the summer tamarisk (see p. 32), roses, some hydrangeas, indigoferas. Late tulips that I have found particularly obliging (and they persist for 20 years or more on a stiffish soil) include the lily-flowered 'White Triumphator' and 'Redshine'; parrots 'Orange Favourite' and 'Texas Gold'; single late 'Mrs John T. Scheepers' (egg-shaped, yellow), 'Dillenburg' (orange) and 'Halcro' (soft red with a touch of pink).

Some of the summer flowering bulbs have lank, decaying foliage at, or soon after, flowering and while it may not hurt to cut it down as soon as flowering is over, it also helps to place them well into your border so that their leaves are hidden by the plants or shrubs in front. Thus, the mauve globes of *Allium giganteum* will rise importantly behind and above a solid evergreen screen of, it might be, *Cistus × corbariensis*, which itself opens pink buds into white flowers in early summer but is still a handsome bush in the depths of winter. The allium's dying foliage is all at ground level.

The early summer flowering *Gladiolus byzantinus*, with magenta spikes, can nestle up against something like border phloxes, whose growth will soon expand and fill in where you have removed the gladiolus evidence. Try and use the kinds with rather light spikes that do not flop around unless staked individually.

Montbretias, now called *Crocosmia*, can make permanent

66

groups like any perennial and flower at the height of summer. *Alstroemeria ligtu* hybrids are a special case. They carry a wonderful display of azalea-like blossom in late June and early July. After that they quickly become an eyesore but because their tubers go deep into the soil, you can plant above them with a late summer replacement, as it might be *Lobelia* 'Queen Victoria', *Salvia patens* or African marigolds held in reserve (they will move from the open ground). All you have to do by way of preparation is to give a sharp tug to all the old alstroemeria stems. They break cleanly, 6 in. (15 cm) or so below the soil surface, leaving the area clear.

Galtonia candicans, the Cape hyacinth, is stiff, with a naked stem to 4 ft (1.2 m) high with its waxy white bells in July-August. When I have planted it well into a border it seems to like to seed itself into the marginal parts and I believe in taking a hint. Try planting it sporadically, rather than in a heavy clump, so that it mixes in with plants mentioned earlier that also go well together: *Eryngium giganteum, Lychnis coronaria, Fuchsia magellanica* 'Versicolor'. The odd plant of sea lavender, *Limonium latifolium*, with a haze of mauve blossom in August above heavy green leaves, would work in here well, also.

The only lilies that I find persist through the years in my heavy slug-infested soil are the purple and white martagons (*Lilium martagon* and *L. m.* 'Album'), and the tall apricot-coloured *L. henryi. Lilium regale*, with its scented white trumpets in July, is excellent on lighter soils. Don't mass any of these, or you'll notice they're doing nothing for you too much of the time. Interplant low shrubs and perennials with them. You can insert an informal line of them behind hostas, whose foliage will spread into their positions at a lowish level.

Of the autumn flowering bulbs, I would not be without some clumps of colchicums. They flower in August-September and their big glossy leaves are lush and handsome in spring. As they yellow, in late May or early June, you must cut them away, before you start grumbling at their unsightliness, and you can either interplant them for the next two or three months with a quick-developing annual like *Dimorphotheca* or *Brachycome* (the Swan river daisy), or allow neighbouring grey-leaved foliage plants of a rambling habit to fill in of their own accord. *Artemisia canescens* (hardy) or *Helichrysum petiolatum* (tender) would meet the occasion.

Nerine × *bowdenii* needs no special baking to make it flower and its pink umbels on 18 in. (45 cm) stems are cheering in September-October. I interplant them with the purple michaelmas daisy, *Aster amellus* 'Violet Queen', which grows to the same height or slightly under and also flowers in autumn. But these will be summer passengers. You may have a brighter idea.

Tender Perennials

This class of plant has to be overwintered under cover or, if left out, its owner must appreciate that a calculated risk is being taken. Safe overwintering will either be by the storage, generally in darkness, of a fleshy, nutrient-rich root or rhizome; or by taking cuttings in the autumn and keeping them under frost-free glass. Sometimes an entire shrubby plant is lifted and returned to the safety of a greenhouse, but this is expensive in terms of space as against the cuttings method, which allows old plants to be discarded. Besides which you rejuvenate your stock by starting again from cuttings rather than saving a woody old lag which may well have lost its zest for growing strongly.

Many of these tender perennials have a prolonged season of flowering or of foliage glamour. They may introduce colours, like red, which are in short supply among the hardies. And they have a lushness which contributes an air of summer opulence to your border.

Dahlias are the most obvious example. Rather than dot them about in any gap that seems to be available at planting time in late spring, but which often does not exist in reality once the border has grown, make special provision for them so that there is space to plant them in groups of one variety, just as you would phloxes or delphiniums.

Dahlias need stout stakes, one to each plant, and stakes are not beautiful objects. Insist that they are of a neutral colour, not that virulent, unnatural shade of green imparted by wood preserving 'Cuprinol' as sometimes sold. Clear 'Cuprinol' is also available and is colourless. Again, it is preferable to have your dahlias growing strongly in their positions before you stake them. That cuts down on the time it will take them to conceal their stakes altogether.

Their tubers in winter need to be stored in a cold but frost free place, as you would potatoes. If their tubers are spindly, not plump, at lifting, they are all to liable to shrivel and it is safer to box them up in old potting soil and give them a watering through the dormant season, say once a week.

This is always the treatment for *Salvia patens*, which makes a cluster of thin tubers. When you see them beginning to sprout in spring, either plant them out or, if the place is occupied, place their box in a cold frame in a light spot. This salvia normally has deep blue flowers on a 2 ft (60 cm) plant, and there is also a Cambridge blue strain. It can alternatively be raised from seed and treated as an annual.

Cannas make fleshy rhizomes in the autumn. Lift their clumps entire and pack them with some extra soil into a deep wooden box. Don't let them dry right out. The clumps, if huge or if you want more stock, can be broken up at planting out in June, by which time they will be growing strongly and have plenty of roots. Cannas are splendid foliage plants, green, purple or variegated, and those with large silken flowers in shades of red, pink or yellow, will do you proud in a hot season. They need no staking.

You can also make special provision, in your border, for those tender perennials which are propagated from cuttings (say 10 to a 3½ in. (9 cm) pot) and overwintered like that, potting them off individually in the spring and hardening them up in a cold frame. As an example, I recently had a patch at the front of my border of a *Verbena* × *hybrida* clone 'Pink Bouquet', with a rosy red bedding *Penstemon*, 'Drinkstone Red', behind it. They were taking the place of *Monarda* 'Cambridge Scarlet', which I had lost in the winter. Verbenas can be raised from seed, but the named clones are sometimes superior to a mixed batch of seedlings, and these must be raised from cuttings. Same story with the penstemons. But they will sometimes survive the winter, in which case the technique is to cut them very hard back in April, when you see new growth appearing at the base. They will then flower to beat the band in early summer, but not a lot thereafter. It might be worth replacing them with late-sown annuals in July.

Various daisies are included among tender perennials. *Chrysanthemum frutescens*, the Paris daisy, has colourful clones such as 'Jamaica Primrose' and the pink, anemone-centred 'Vancouver'. *Chrysanthemum foeniculaceum* is a white daisy but with excellent lacy foliage of glaucous hue. *Euryops chrysanthemoides* is covered with daisies all summer of a clear, sharp yellow. *Osteospermum* 'Buttermilk' is one of several South African daisies, somewhat bushy in habit, this one pale yellow. That known as 'Ecklonis Prostrata' is mat-forming and will creep out over paving from a marginal planting. White, blue-eyed daisies with a mauve reverse.

The rambling habit of *Helichrysum petiolatum*, with felted heart-shaped leaves, makes an ideal gap filler of this foliage plant. Another that gives quick returns is the grey, double-comb-leaved *Senecio leucostachys*.

The most important biennials for mixed border work are foxgloves, mulleins, stocks, sweet williams, honesty, forget-me-nots and evening primroses. I exclude canterbury bells (*Campanula medium*) because they go over so quickly and the dead blooms hang on. First to flower are *Myosotis*, the forget-me-nots and they have a long season, up to the very end of May, at which stage you should pull out all those that are still visible and forget (sorry, yes, forget) about those which have become engulfed in rapidly growing perennials. Forget-me-nots are, indeed, most useful for filling in between plants of phloxes, for instance, which will not themselves be inhibited by their proximity. But watch it when myosotis seed themselves (as, in the mixed border context, we depend upon them to do after the first introduction) among small plants which they can easily engulf and kill. When overhauling your border in autumn or spring, therefore, weed out any plants that you can see will later be a nuisance. Leave those that will extend your border's season. When they're flowering, swivel a sharp eye on to them again, making sure there's no mischief afoot.

Lunaria annua, which we call honesty, the American money plant, likewise. They self-sow like crazy but, being shade tolerant, give excellent value beneath and among shrubs, as it might be lilac or the suckering *Clerodendron bungei*, which carries domes of rich carmine, scented flowers above luxuriant heart-shaped foliage in late summer and autumn. The white honesty and the two variegated kinds, one with white flowers, the other with mauve, but both with a pale cream variegation, show up especially well in shade. But you must keep them separate, otherwise they will not come true from seed. All flower in May.

Foxgloves, *Digitalis purpurea*, are likewise excellent value in shade, beneath tall shrubs or trees, but they are June flowering. You can allow them to maintain themselves by self-sowing but this becomes unsatisfactory over a period of years because they tend to revert to the wild, pinkish purple colouring, which does not show up too well from a distance in the garden and clashes abominably with any orange flowers. The apricot and white digitalis strains would be my first choice, although the giant spotted kinds are great fun. I do not consider that the Excelsior hybrids, which display their flowers horizontally, have any particular advantages. Foxgloves passing out of bloom are ugly and the plants should be pulled out as this stage approaches. You need annuals in reserve to take their place.

I believe in raising foxgloves, sweet williams and mulleins properly, so as to obtain the finest plants. Sow in a pot in April under cold glass; prick off the seedlings, 28 or 40 to a tray. Then line them out, 15 in. (38 cm) apart in a spare plot for the summer. Move them into their flowering positions in the autumn.

Sweet williams, *Dianthus barbatus*, are all too often scattered about through a border and then left to run to seed after flowering, which is most unsightly, since their season ends in the second half of July and they need a follow-on. This is much more convenient to provide if the sweet williams are given a patch in your border to themselves. You can interplant them with tulips. Lift the whole lot in late July, harvesting the bulbs and discarding the sweet willies and replant with an annual or bedding dahlias, sown in May. If you sow sweet williams too late, they only flower at half cock in the following year. April is best, and the plants, when growing them on, can be sprayed with a copper fungicide to prevent an attack of rust on their foliage.

The most dramatic of the biennial mulleins is *Verbascum olympicum*, which soars to 8 ft (2.4 m) (give it a stake in case of high winds) and has a great branching candelabrum of yellow blossom. Be sure to spray (or handpick twice daily for a week) the handsome but destructive caterpillars of the mullein shark moth while they are still small, in early June. *Verbascum bombyciferum*, also called 'Silver Lining', or 'Silver Spire', has beautiful, felted, pale grey foliage which is at its most striking in the rosette stage in the first year and as the spike is running up in the late spring of the second. In flower it is less well balanced than V. *olympicum* (and so is V. *phlomoides*, which is sometimes sold as V. *olympicum*).

A number of the evening primroses are biennials and can be allowed to self-sow. The least weedy looking in habit, indeed it can be statuesque, is *Oenothera erythrosepala*, sometimes known as *O. lamarckiana*. It grows to 6 ft (1.8 m) and opens its great bowl-shaped yellow chalices at dusk. They last into the next forenoon.

Stocks (*Matthiola*) of the Brompton strain can be bedded into your border from a late spring sowing, in the autumn and will be at their best the following late May and June (to be followed, of course, by annuals). Their scent is delicious and the single-flowered kinds mix pleasantly with doubles. They are happiest on light soils. On heavy ground they tend to go down to botrytis in the spring of the second year; it is worth treating them with carbendazim in the New Year, again in March.

Lupins can be treated as biennials in the same way as foxgloves, sweet williams and stocks, being followed by annuals.

Annuals

Few annuals have much structure to them (*Nicotiana sylvestris, Polygonum orientale* and *Cleome spinosa* are obvious exceptions) and a bed or border devoted to them alone suffers from this defect. Also it has a tendency to pack too much colour, indigestibly, into a small space. In a mixed border their colour may have great advantages, while other kinds of plants will provide the elements of shape, texture and solidity.

Tall annuals are useful for replacing the biennials I have just been describing when they have done their turn. Also for filling a big gap left by a shrub that has died unexpectedly. My enormous specimen of *Solanum crispum* 'Glasnevin', with a host of mauve potato flowers in summer, died one year after flowering, without leaving the customary suicide note. I have since filled in with annuals and biennials and so enjoy the gap that I have no immediate intention of a permanent planting. That is one of the lovely things about annuals and biennials. You can change your mind so quickly about which to use and about changes to make next year. Happy armchair hours with catalogues arise from this plotting in the depths of winter when your mind needs lifting out of the present. Some people do it with travel brochures. Gardeners can bring exotica to their own doorsteps.

Nicotiana sylvestris, with large, rich green paddle leaves and heads of long-tubed white flowers, deliciously night scented, is an excellent follow-on to foxglove or honesty in a rather shady but moist and well fed situation.

To replace lupins and verbascums in an open site, I choose from a number of favourites. *Tithonia rotundifolia* 'Torch' is like a giant zinnia with glowing orange flowers. The dwarfer 'Goldfinger' has not nearly its style or presence. *Cosmos bipinnatus*, with its feathery foliage on a 4–5 ft (1.2–1.5 m) plant (give each a cane and a tie and space them at 2 ft (60 cm)), comes in various pink and carmine shades, usually mixed, but is most attractive, I think, in the pure white 'Purity', which also has paler green leaves.

Lavatera trimestris 'Loveliness' and 'Tanagra' are excellent pink mallows but a trifle brash in colouring. The soft rosy red *Malope trifida* 'Grandiflora' is a close relation. The green calyx shines like stained glass window slits in the base of each funnel flower. Stake as for cosmos, as also the sweet scabious *Scabiosa atropurpurea*.

This is best sown in early autumn and overwintered in individual pots under cold glass, planting out in spring, thus bringing forward the onset of its otherwise tardy flowering to July. The spider flower, *Cleome spinosa*, has palmate leaves like a horsechesnut and pink, white or bright mauve flowers on an indefinitely lengthening stem that continues over a long period. Never starve this as a seedling, or it won't recover.

Polygonum orientale has dropped out of the lists so I must write about it to get it back. It makes an elegant 4 ft (1.2 m) plant (but beware slugs) of a branching habit covered with drooping spikelets of deep carmine flowers.

The castor oil, *Ricinus communis*, is grown for its bold, palmate leaves which are most striking in the purple-leaved 'Gibsonii'. In a warm summer this may grow to 5–6 ft (1.5–1.8 m). Much depends on the season (as also for tithonias).

Dahlias treated as annuals also make excellent follow-ons. If the plants are not needed until late June or up to the end of July, you must delay your sowings till some time in May and keep the young plants happy by potting them individually, even into 5 in. (12 cm) pots if the wait is a long one. Then, when you do plant them out, they will be ready to go into immediate action.

African marigolds (*Tagetes erecta*), the large growing, widely branching kinds like 'Climax' and 'Toreador', are of special value in a mixed border because they are imposing plants (unlike the Inca series with large blooms on a small plant, which looks totally unbalanced). From a late April or May sowing under cold glass they can be lined out in a spare plot until needed and, given a good soaking before and after, moved into their final positions as large plants already coming into flower.

There are many delightful, natural looking annuals to use near a border's margin. Direct sowings are seldom as satisfactory as raising plants under controlled conditions initially (sun heat is quite sufficient and an April sowing early enough), pricking out the seedlings into, for preference, deep boxes, not more than 40, often only 28 to a box. You can use soilless or John Innes composts, both of which will be weed-free. In the latter case, sow and prick out into J.I. potting compost No. 1 (the seed compost is necessary only for early sowings when days are short and sunlight weak).

Of the shorter annuals with a long flowering season I would recommend the bushy, 12 in. (30 cm), *Cuphea miniata* 'Firefly', which is pinky-red and has a prettily shaped flower. *Anagallis linifolia* in its blue form is as intensely coloured as a gentian and often mistaken for one. It is almost prostrate and grows about 6 in. (15 cm) high. *Calceolaria mexicana* is an elegant species, to 2 ft (60 cm) smothered in flattened pouches of a nice acid, palish yellow. Once grown it will self-sow year after year. *Brachycome iberidifolia* is the Swan river daisy, usually seen in mixtures: blue, purple, mauve and white; swarms of blossom on 9 in. (23 cm) plants with fine-spun leaves.

Other self-seeders include *Nemophila maculata*, a hardy annual whose seedlings appear in the autumn. Bowl-shaped, palest mauve flowers in May, each petal having a deep purple spot at its tip. Love-in-a-mist, *Nigella damascena*, deserves to be grown in a pure blue strain, as we have few enough blues, but the purplish *N. hispanica* is a striking species. *Alonsoa warscewiczii* looks less weedy in its 18 in. (45 cm) tall compact strain. It has pale scarlet flowers over a long season. The annual grass, *Briza maxima*, with flowers like dangling lockets, should not be omitted though its self-sown seedlings will need thinning out each autumn.

Like the forget-me-nots, these self-sowers can weave in among other plants, weeding out only those that will be a nuisance to a more permanent neighbour; or they can grow over the bare patch left in summer by bulbs like colchicums and sternbergias that are resting.

ENVOI

Mixed borders, once you get the hang of the idea, become a way of life and there are many directions in which you can steer your own particular craft. Your temperament will decide the direction taken and you will be revealing a piece of yourself through your art, which gardening is.

This section makes suggestions and offers help, from my experience, of ways and means. Once the reader has got his own ideas, he will be able to dispense with me altogether, but I hope now and again to be allowed to see and enjoy the results.

Opposite: Autumn foliage colours give interest to the border at the end of the year. In the foreground liriope is in full flower

Plants for Shade

FAY SHARMAN

A collection of hostas growing in a shady courtyard with
Hydrangea anomala petiolaris clothing the house wall

Introduction

Shade is an integral part of the natural landscape, where trees, shrubs, perennials, bulbs and grasses coexist at different levels in a harmonious whole. The most effective garden is based on the same principle, of planting in layers, and contains a mixture of sun- and shade-loving plants. A totally shadeless garden would be a dull and artificial place, lacking the subtle effects, the contrasts between light and dark and the sense of tranquillity which shade can provide.

There are many plants which actually prefer shade, including not only numerous shrubs, but herbaceous perennials, bulbs, ferns and annuals. Although often less flamboyant than sun-lovers, they compensate in various ways – with delicately coloured flowers, a long season of bloom, attractive foliage or fruits, a graceful habit. In addition to the active shade-lovers, some versatile plants succeed in sun or shade, even if they may be less floriferous in the latter. The Mexican orange blossom, *Choisya ternata*, for example, is content with a sunless corner or against a south-facing wall. However, there is no point trying resolutely sun-loving plants in shade: they will soon show their dislike of such a position by becoming pale and drawn, with lanky thin stems, large floppy leaves and few, if any, flowers.

Shade can be a great asset in the garden, offering the opportunity to grow a host of delightful plants. However, there are several degrees of shade and, the denser it is, the more restricted the choice of plants. While many woodland plants enjoy the dappled shade of trees and others appreciate partial shade, where they are protected from the hottest sun, very few can survive in deep permanent shade. Similarly, certain plants may grow well in the open shade of a wall or building, but be unable to tolerate the heavy direct shade beneath a tree, which is made worse by drip from the leaves and competition from the roots. This is where shade can be a challenge to the gardener, not a blessing, and it is a common problem in the typical small garden of today.

Opposite: *Oxalis acetosella* 'Rosea', a pink-flowered wood sorrel, thrives in dappled shade

Shade in the Garden

ASSESSING THE SITUATION

It is rarely possible to reduce the amount of shade in a garden, where this is caused by existing features such as walls, buildings or tall overhanging trees. In a small town or suburban garden, some parts inevitably receive little or no sunshine.

If you are buying a house, it is important to check the orientation of its garden. Remember that the extent of shade varies considerably according to the time of year and that, as the day progresses from sunrise to sunset, there is a continual movement of shadows. It is always worth observing a new garden through the seasons before deciding what can be grown where.

The selection and positioning of plants requires forward planning. A frequent mistake is to underestimate the rate of growth of a tree or shrub and to find that, within a few years, its shadow has encroached on a previously sunny bed. Regional differences in climate should also be taken into account. The south and east of Britain tend to be hotter and drier than the rest of the country: here plants may rely on shade to supply the cool moist conditions they need, whereas in the colder or wetter north and west they can thrive in full sun.

A shady garden can be just as rewarding as a sunny one, if you make the most of each area by using suitable plants – climbers to enhance a north-facing wall, frost-tender shrubs taking advantage of the shelter of an enclosed space, woodlanders in the filtered light beneath trees. A damp place in the shade could be converted into a bog garden and, as a last resort, there are some cosmetic solutions for those really awkward dark spots, where almost nothing will grow.

TYPES OF SHADE

It is extremely hard to define degrees of shade, especially since these are linked to other factors like soil conditions and the nature of the site. However, it is useful to distinguish initially three broad categories, which will have a bearing on the choice of plants:

1 *Permanent shade*
a) A dark corner or similar enclosed spot which is always in shade, because the sun is excluded by nearby obstacles, such as a building, wall or fence, an evergreen hedge or tree.

The beautiful 'Maigold' is one of several roses which can be grown on a north-facing wall

b) A north-facing border or wall which experiences constant shade but is open to the sky.

2 *Partial shade*
An area which is in shadow for part of the day as the sun moves across the sky.

3 *Dappled shade*
An area beneath a high thin canopy of deciduous trees, whose leaves and branches filter the sunlight.

SHADE FROM TREES

As major sources of shade, trees present special problems. One of the most serious is that their roots rob the surrounding soil of the moisture and food needed by other plants. Beech and birch are notoriously greedy, although the deeper-rooting oak is more accommodating. Hedges, particularly privet with its invasive roots, can make planting equally difficult. In all these cases, thorough preparation of the soil is vital if plants are to succeed.

Trees cast shade to varying degrees. There is the perpetual deep shade of a dense evergreen tree, such as holly, and the summer-time shade of a deciduous tree, which may be heavy or light according to the size, shape and quantity of leaves. Small leaves and open branches produce the pleasant dappled shade favoured by many plants. On the other hand, large leaves or dense over-lapping foliage, of horse chestnut or beech for example, effectively block out the light and also allow very little rain to penetrate. Few plants will grow in the heavy shade beneath them.

An additional factor is the height and form of the tree. A tall up-right tree with a straight trunk will admit more light, as well as rain, than a spreading tree with low branches, to the greater bene-fit of plants underneath. Light can be improved to a certain extent by removing some of the lower branches of a tree and thinning out the crown, but care must be taken not to spoil the overall ap-pearance. The distance between trees, too, will obviously in-fluence the amount of light reaching the ground.

With deciduous trees, the timing of leaf development is yet another consideration. A horse chestnut will normally have completed its canopy of foliage by mid-May, so that very little apart from spring-flowering bulbs can be planted below it, where-as a walnut will not be in full leaf until July, enabling a wider variety of plants to be grown. Similarly, some trees keep their foliage later in the season than others, which affects the use of the ground beneath. When the leaves fall each autumn, they supply valuable organic material to the soil, from which lesser plants can profit, although there is an attendant risk of smothering if the leaves are large and heavy like those of the sycamore. Drip from trees can also cause damage.

SOIL

Closely linked with the basic types of shade are the soil condi-tions, which may range from dry to moist and acid to alkaline. These too will determine the choice of plants.

Probably the easiest shady place to plant is the edge of a pond or bank of a stream, where there is a plentiful supply of water. Many plants revel in such a situation, among them primulas and hostas. In fact, most shade-lovers prefer to be moist and cool. The pro-blem areas are those of dry shade and unfortunately they tend to be in the majority – beside walls or high buildings and under over-hanging eaves, where little rain reaches the soil, and beneath trees or near hedges, whose roots compete for any rainfall which does penetrate.

The goat's beard, *Aruncus dioicus*, is a spectacular plant for dappled shade, particularly in moist soil

Dry soils in shade need thorough preparation before planting, incorporating as much bulky organic material as possible to retain moisture. Home-made compost, leafmould or peat are suitable and should be dug into the top layer of soil. This preliminary digging and improvement of the soil is particularly important on new sites, where the earth has often become dry and compacted by machinery and may be full of builder's rubble.

Aquilegia long-spurred hybrids compose a pleasant picture in shade

A mulch of similar material, after planting, will also help to conserve moisture in the soil. It should be spread in a layer about 2 in. (5 cm) thick, tucking it between the plants, and is best applied annually in late February or early March.

Cultivation of the soil is not always possible, in rooty ground under a tree, for instance, or on a steep bank. Here the answer could be to clear the area with a contact non-persistent weedkiller (for instance, paraquat and diquat) and then plant vigorous ground-covering plants, such as periwinkle, *Vinca major*, or the rose of Sharon, *Hypericum calycinum*.

The chemical composition of the soil also plays a part in the selection of plants. The degree of acidity is expressed by the pH scale: a neutral soil has a pH of 7, below 7 is acid and above alkaline. Soil pH can be measured with a simple soil-testing kit. The majority of plants enjoy a neutral to slightly acid soil, although many are tolerant of a wide range of conditions. It is only the extremes which cause difficulty. Fortunately, however, some of the most beautiful shade-lovers require and thrive on acid soil, notably rhododendrons and camellias. At the other end of the scale, plants like clematis, osmanthus and the invaluable *Choisya ternata* succeed in shade on alkaline soil, even in a shallow dry soil over chalk.

Choosing Plants for Shade

The following suggestions for plants to grow in various types of shade are by no means exhaustive, but may be taken as representative. In many cases, the categories overlap and it is often worth experimenting with plants in different situations.

The plants are divided into two groups – shrubs first and then other plants, including herbaceous perennials, bulbs, ferns and grasses – and are listed under their botanical names in alphabetical order. It is not possible to give precise dimensions for plants, as they will vary to some extent according to conditions, and the measurements are intended merely as a guide.

PERMANENT DEEP SHADE

Dark corners, narrow passages between houses, basements and other enclosed spaces, where the sun never penetrates, are a common problem. This all-the-year-round shade can be suffocating to plants, particularly if, as often happens, the soil is dry and lifeless or dank and mossy. The advice given on thorough soil preparation is all the more applicable in such conditions and the addition of moisture-retentive material is vital.

An area like this is so definite that it basically dictates the range of plants which can be grown there. However, various devices can help to improve appearances. Painting the walls a paler colour or white brings light to a dark corner and provides a good background for foliage and flowers, showing off both shapes and colours. Light-coloured paving and white trellis could also be introduced. Similarly, plants with variegated or yellow-flushed leaves will brighten the effect, although in some cases the markings may fade in the restricted light. Silver foliage plants, unfortunately, rarely succeed in shade.

Building a raised bed is another idea if one wants to get the most out of a confined area. It adds a new dimension of interest, breaking up any flatness and detracting from the apparent height of surrounding walls. It has practical advantages too, where the existing soil is worn out or poorly drained, since the bed can be filled with fresh soil and provision made for correct drainage. It is surprising how much extra light can often be obtained by raising a bed a few feet above ground level. A raised bed can be planted in the ordinary way with shrubs, herbaceous perennials and annuals, or it can be devoted to alpine and dwarf plants whose charms are most appreciated close to (see p.130 for suggestions). Perhaps the quickest, though not necessarily the cheapest, solution for difficult and dark places is to use containers (see p.131). As well as being decorative in their own right, these broaden the scope and enable one to grow plants which might otherwise fail in such adverse conditions.

(In addition to the suggestions below, see *Euonymus, Gaultheria Ribes, Sarcococca.*)

Shrubs

Aucuba

A medium-sized evergreen shrub 6–10 ft (1.8–3 m) high, *A. japonica* has leaves either dark green, variegated or spotted with yellow, depending on the form. 'Crotonifolia' has handsome golden-variegated leaves. Female plants produce attractive red berries in winter, if grown with males. The aucuba succeeds in dense and dry shade and is excellent in town gardens.

Buxus

The common box, *B. sempervirens*, will tolerate deep shade and makes a useful evergreen shrub or hedge, thriving on chalky soils. There are numerous cultivars, ranging in size from dwarf to large and some having variegated or coloured foliage. They include the tall 'Handsworthensis', with thick, dark green leaves, and the popular 'Gold Tip', with yellow-tipped leaves.

Choisya

The Mexican orange blossom, *C. ternata*, is a most versatile evergreen shrub, equally at home in sun or shade, although less so under trees. Of rounded bushy habit, it grows 8–10 ft (2.5–3 m) high and bears clusters of fragrant white blossom in April and May, sometimes continuing until October. It is also extremely hardy.

× Fatshedera lizei

This hybrid between *Fatsia japonica* and ivy (probably the Irish ivy, *Hedera, helix* 'Hibernica') is a handsome evergreen shrub or semi-climber up to 10 ft (3 m), with large, leathery, lustrous, dark green leaves like those of the ivy. It is a tough and vigorous plant, invaluable for dense dry shade, especially in towns. It usually

Above: The rose of Sharon, *Hypericum calycinum* (left), is an invaluable groundcover; *Ilex aquifolium* 'Silver Milkboy' (right), an attractive variegated holly

Below: The Oregon grape, *Mahonia aquifolium* (left), an outstanding shrub for shade; *Skimmia japonica* (right) contributes interest for much of the year

needs supporting with a stake, but can be kept more bushy by pinching out when young.

Fatsia

Well known as a houseplant, *F. japonica*, may grow 6–10 ft (1.8–3 m) high and has huge, lobed, shiny, dark green leaves and, in autumn, rounded heads of milky white flowers. It is a striking evergreen for a sheltered spot in shade.

Hedera

The familiar ivies are invaluable evergreen climbers or ground-cover for dark spots, particularly in town gardens. The common ivy, *H. helix*, will succeed in almost any situation and soil, rapidly clothing a shady wall or carpeting bare ground where little else would survive. Many forms are available, with plain green, variegated or variously coloured leaves of different shapes.

Hypericum

The rose of Sharon, *H. calycinum*, is a vigorous, widespreading, low shrub, no more than 1–1½ ft (30–45 cm) high, with masses of golden yellow flowers from June to September. It is an ideal groundcover, even in full shade and dry soil. Once established, it is best cut back to near ground level in February each year to keep it compact (see p.87). The tutsan, *H. androsaemum*, is another useful member of the genus for dry shady places. Only 2–3 ft (60–90 cm) high and across, it has large deciduous leaves, small yellow flowers from June to September and black fruits. It seems indifferent to soil conditions and seeds itself with abandon.

Ilex

With its dark green, prickly leaves, dense pyramidal habit and red berries in winter (if male and female plants are grown together), the common holly, *I. aquifolium*, is one of the best evergreens. It is quite happy in heavy shade, although berrying less freely, and may be grown as a small tree, reaching a height of 30–40 ft (9–12 m) and with a spread of some 20 ft (6 m), or used to form a hedge. It does not take kindly to transplanting and is most succesful from self- sown seed. There are a large number of cultivars of different habits, leaf shapes and colours. Many of them are variegated (see p.87), although some of these are inclined to revert.

Lonicera

Of the shrubby honeysuckles, the semi-evergreen L. *pileata* is a fine groundcover plant, particularly for shady banks and dry areas. Only about 3 ft (90 cm) high and spreading, its main attraction is the neat, dark green, shining foliage, although insignificant whitish flowers appear in May, sometimes followed by violet berries.

Mahonia

The Oregon grape, M. *aquifolium*, is a small evergreen shrub 3–5 ft (90 cm–1.5 m) high and as wide, which covers the ground by means of suckers. It should be cut back in spring, just after flowering, to stop it becoming straggly. The glossy, dark green leaves, made up of leaflets, turn purplish red in winter, while the rich yellow flowers may start to open in February, reaching a peak in April and May. Abundant blue-black berries are also produced. This attractive plant is not fussy about soil or situation and will do well in all but the densest shade (see p.87).

Pachysandra

The evergreen P. *terminalis* is a semi-woody plant, less than 1 ft (30 cm) high. It is an efficient carpeter in shade, developing into a solid low mass, and has unusual diamond-shaped leaves of light green, with inconspicuous flowers in spring. It tolerates dry soil, but is not good on chalk.

Prunus

The cherry laurel or common laurel, P. *laurocerasus*, is one of the most shade-tolerant evergreens and will thrive in almost any soil. The dwarf forms, such as 'Otto Luyken', 'Schipkaensis' and 'Zabeliana' are all about 3 ft (90 cm) high, with a spread of 5 ft (1.5 m) or more, and can be recommended as groundcover. They have narrow, shining green leaves and spikes of small white flowers in spring.

Rubus

Although not outstandingly ornamental in flower, several members of this genus (which includes the raspberry and blackberry) are good ground-covering plants for sun or shade. Especially useful for a dry shady place and very fast growing is the semi-evergreen R. *tricolor*. It is about 1 ft (30 cm) high, with long, trailing, bristly stems and dark green leaves, felted white beneath. Solitary white flowers appear in July and are followed by bright red fruits, which are worth eating.

Ruscus

Butcher's broom, *R. aculeatus*, is a small evergreen shrub 2–3 ft (60–90 cm) high, spreading by suckers and making thick clumps. It bears bright red berries, if male and female are grown together, and is an indispensable plant for deep shade and poor conditions.

Sambucus

The native common elder, *S. nigra*, is easily recognized in the countryside by the heads of scented creamy flowers in June and later the heavy bunches of shiny black fruits (both of which are used to make wine). A deciduous shrub or tree some 15–30 ft (4.5–9 m) tall, it is often considered a weed in gardens because of its propensity to reproduce itself from seed. However, it is a real utility plant for difficult sites and will grow in damp dark corners and on extremely chalky soils.

Skimmia

The adaptable *S. japonica* will flourish in various degrees of shade, in dry conditions and on acid or alkaline soil. It is a compact evergreen bush, 3–4 ft (90 cm–1.2 m) high and the same width. The fragrant white blossom in April and May is succeeded by round, bright red fruits (when male and female plants are grouped), which persist through the winter (see p.87).

Symphoricarpus

The snowberry, *S. albus* var. *laevigatus* (*S. rivularis*), is a vigorous suckering shrub 4–5 ft (1.2–1.5 m) high. Its chief merit is the large, pure white berries, which are freely carried from October into the new year and add a touch of brightness to the winter months. It is a popular choice for dark out-of-the-way places in the garden, where its rampant growth will not cause trouble. It forms dense thickets and, although deciduous, can be an effective screen.

Taxus

The English yew, *T. baccata*, with its small, narrow, dark green leaves and red fruits on female plants, is a useful evergreen for shady conditions. It is usually seen as a tree some 40 ft (12 m) tall or as a formal clipped hedge, but there are numerous cultivars of varying habits and foliage colours. They include some low prostrate kinds, like 'Repandens', which are superb groundcover for deep shade. The yew is suitable for almost any type of reasonably drained soil.

Viburnum

The laurustinus, V. tinus, is a deservedly popular evergreen shrub, with masses of dark green, glossy foliage and a long succession of pink-budded white flowers in flat heads from November to April. 'Eve Price' is a delightful form with pinkish blooms. Growing about 8–10 ft (2.5–3 m) high, it is a multi-purpose plant for sun or shade, although flowering less freely in very dense shade. It may also be used as a screen.

Vinca

Few plants are so accommodating and decorative as the periwinkles, both of them first-class groundcover for steep banks, waste ground and other awkward situations in shade and excellent for town gardens. The greater periwinkle, V. major, is a rampant trailing shrub and roots as it spreads. It has dark green leaves, or leaves boldly edged in creamy white in the often seen 'Variegata', and bright blue flowers opening in April, sometimes continuing at odd times until September. The lesser periwinkle, V. minor, is similar, but smaller and neater, making a low thick carpet. Neither flower as well in shade, but the mats of evergreen foliage are ample compensation.

Perennials

Asplenium

The hart's tongue fern, A. scolopendrium (Phyllitis scolopendrium) is a native evergreen fern with bright green, broad, strap-shaped fronds, 1–2 ft (60–90 cm) tall. It revels in shade, reproducing itself readily, and will grow in any soil, including chalk, but must have some moisture (see p.92).

Convallaria

The lily of the valley, C. majalis, is an unpredictable yet highly desirable plant, with the gracefully hanging, scented, white, bell-shaped flowers in spring set off by fresh green foliage. It seems to

The hart's tongue fern, *Asplenium scolopendrium*, is distinctive for its undulating fronds

thrive in many different soils, even in town gardens, preferring shade or half-shade. Once established, it is a vigorous spreader and, as the leaves last until autumn, it makes an efficient ground-cover about 9 in. (23 cm) high.

Dryopteris

The common native fern, *D. filix-mas*, known as the male fern, grows wild in all sorts of unlikely places and happily accepts both dry impoverished ground and heavy shade. It unfolds into large, dull green, divided fronds of elegant upright habit, eventually reaching a height of 4 ft (1.2 m), and soon colonizes the surrounding soil.

Euphorbia

A low evergreen perennial about 2 ft (60 cm) high, *E. robbiae* has rosettes of dark green leaves on purplish stems and greenish yellow flowers in spring. With its creeping roots, it is a reliable and quick groundcover for poor shady spots.

Iris

The long-suffering *I. foetidissima*, stinking gladwyn, will withstand deep shade and dry soil of any kind, though doing best in a moist well-drained position. Growing to some 1½ ft (45 cm) high, it forms clumps of rich green, arching, evergreen leaves, with bluish lilac flowers in early summer, followed by striking orange seed heads. These last into winter and are good for cutting. 'Citrina' is an improved form, with larger yellow flowers and bigger seed pods.

Saxifraga

The familiar London pride, *S. × urbium*, has rosettes of spoon-shaped leaves, from which arise loose panicles of starry pink flowers on 1 ft (30 cm) stems in early summer. It is a compact groundcover for permanently shady areas, provided the soil is moist, and good in town gardens, as the name implies.

Waldsteinia ternata, a delightful evergreen carpeter for heavy shade

Symphytum

The ground-covering comfrey, *S. grandiflorum*, is a rapid spreader no more than 10 in. (25 cm) high. It develops into a close mat of foliage, producing pale yellow, tubular flowers in spring. It likes shade and does best in a moist heavy soil, but will also cope with relatively dry conditions.

Trachystemon

Another member of the borage family, as is comfrey, *T. orientale* is a vigorous perennial for any shady place large enough to contain it. The huge, hairy, heart-shaped leaves emerge in late spring and are preceded by purplish blue flowers, the overall height being 1–1½ ft (30–45 cm) and the width 2 ft (60 cm).

Waldsteinia

The pretty little *W. ternata* creates thick mats of evergreen strawberry foliage and has golden yellow blooms in April and May. It is content with dry or moist soil, sun or shade, and is restrained enough for the town garden (see p.93).

A NORTH-FACING BORDER

A border facing north and cut off from the sun by intervening obstacles comes under the general heading of permanent shade, except perhaps briefly in midsummer when the sun is highest. However, because of its open aspect, the shade is usually less oppressive than in a dark enclosed area, although this depends on the height and proximity of any buildings or trees. It is often a bleak site, but can be improved by providing shelter in the form of a hedge or screen. The plants already mentioned under permanent shade (pp.85–94) will, of course, do equally well here; and for further suggestions, see *Chaenomeles, Cotoneaster, Garrya, Pyracantha, Rosa* in the next section.

Shrubs

Camellia

The innumerable cultivars of the common camellia, *C. japonica*, are prized not only for their magnificent flowers, from early to late spring, but also for their highly polished, evergreen leaves, which remain decorative all year. Most are medium-sized shrubs 10–12 ft (3–3.5 m) high, although they may become much larger with age. Those with a more compact habit of growth are ideal as free-standing specimens in a north-facing position. This gives protection from early morning sunshine, which can damage the blooms after frost by causing them to thaw too rapidly. Camellias do particularly well in town gardens, where there is less exposure to wind and the risk of frost damage is reduced. Two well-tried favourites are 'Adolphe Audusson' – blood-red semi-double flowers with prominent gold stamens; and 'Alba Plena' – large, double, white flowers on a bushy plant.

The common camellia needs fairly high summer temperatures in order to form buds and for this reason does not succeed in Scotland. A better choice in colder districts are the many *C. × williamsii* hybrids, which flower profusely over a long period, from November to May, and have the added merit of shedding the dead blooms. These include the famous 'Donation' – erect and vigorous, with semi-double, silvery pink flowers in March and April; and 'St Ewe' – single, funnel-shaped, purplish pink flowers and neat upright habit.

All camellias require moist lime-free soil containing peat or leafmould and benefit from regular mulching.

Osmanthus

An evergreen shrub which slowly attains a height of 6–10 ft (1.8–3 m), *O. × burkwoodii* has dark, shining green leaves and clusters of sweet-smelling white flowers in April or May. The holly-like *O. heterophyllus* is a dense bush of similar height, with fragrant white flowers in autumn; there is also a form with variegated leaves. These attractive shrubs make good thick hedges, if required, and are content with shade and a wide range of soils, including shallow chalk.

Paeonia

The shrubby peonies are such magnificent foliage and flowering plants that they amply repay a little extra care. Although perfectly hardy, they need protection from spring frosts, which can damage the young shoots and buds; at the same time, they should not have too warm a position, which would encourage premature growth. A north-facing situation is therefore ideal, with a screen of sacking, if necessary, to shelter them from frost. They do best in a rich, well drained soil.

A deciduous shrub, *P. delavayi* attains a height of 5–6 ft (1.5–1.8 m) and produces deep crimson, cup-shaped flowers with prominent golden anthers in May or June. Its greatest attribute,

Left: The gorgeous blooms of the tree peony, derived from *Paeonia suffruticosa*

Right: *Ribes sanguineum* 'Brocklebankii', a flowering currant with golden yellow foliage

however, is the large, deeply divided, dark green foliage. The same may be said of *P. lutea* var. *ludlowii*, a handsome plant of similar dimensions, whose leaves tend to obscure the golden yellow, saucer-shaped blooms. The many forms of the tree peony, *P. suffruticosa*, grow 4–5 ft (1.2–1.5 m) high and bring an exotic touch to any garden. Enormous single, semi-double or double flowers are borne from late May in a range of colours from white to crimson-purple. (See also p.100 for herbaceous peonies.)

Prunus

As well as the cherry laurel, *P. laurocerasus* (p.89), the Portugal laurel, *P. lusitanica*, is a fine evergreen for growing in shade. It may be allowed to develop into a stately shrub, reaching 15–20 ft (4.5–6 m) high and 12–15 ft (3.5–4.5 m) wide, or can be trained into formal shape or as a hedge. The abundant racemes of scented white blossom in June are shown off by rich green, glossy foliage and followed by small, dark purple fruits. It thrives on all soils.

Ribes

The mountain currant, *R. alpinum*, is very tolerant of shade and not fussy about soil. It is a neat deciduous shrub, some 6–9 ft (1.8–3 m) tall and as much in diameter, with modest, greenish yellow flowers in spring and red berries; the leaves turn yellow in autumn. 'Brocklebankii', a cultivar of the popular flowering currant, *R. sanguineum*, demands a shady place for the sake of its yellow foliage, which tends to burn in full sun. It is a pleasant low-growing shrub, 4–5 ft (1.2–5 m) high, and produces pink flowers in April. The currants are good in town gardens.

Sarcococca

The sarcococcas, relatives of box, provide excellent evergreen groundcover, particularly in the small garden, where their low compact growth is appreciated. About 2 ft (90 cm) high and wide, *S. hookeriana* var. *digyna* has glossy, dark green leaves, white fragrant flowers in winter and black fruits. The similar but dwarfer *S. humilis* suckers to form clumps and bears pinky white flowers in February. Both withstand shade and dry soil.

Viburnum

Another evergreen viburnum suitable for shade, apart from *V. tinus* (p.19), is *V. davidii*, although it is not successful under trees. This wide mound-shaped shrub grows 2–3 ft (60–90 cm) in height and 4–5 ft (1.2–1.5 m) in spread and in June carries flat heads of small white flowers against the dark green, veined leaves. Turquoise-blue berries are produced, if male and female plants are grouped.

Aconitum

The monkshoods, mainly hybrids between *A. napellus* and *A. variegatum*, are stately herbaceous perennials up to 4 ft (1.2 m) tall, with stiff spires of helmeted flowers and glossy, dark green, divided leaves. Blooming in various tones of blue from July to September, they do as well in shade as in full sun. The roots are highly poisonous.

Perennials

Anemone

The Japanese anemone, *A. × hybrida* (*A. japonica* of gardens), is a beautiful perennial for the shady border and does well in town gardens. It multiplies freely once established, does not need staking, despite its height of 2–3 ft (60–90 cm), and flowers at a welcome time in early autumn. The blooms are a delicate rose-pink, although there are several named kinds, ranging from white to pale to deep pink and with semi-double or double flowers (see p.98).

Above: The Japanese anemone, *Anemone × hybrida* (left), an old favourite in gardens; *Bergenia crassifolia* (right), with handsome spoon-shaped leaves

Below: *Helleborus corsicus* (left) flowers early in the year; the double red peony, *Paeonia officinalis* 'Rubra Plena' (right), has been grown since the sixteenth century

Bergenia

The bergenia species and hybrids offer a rich variety of colours in their large rounded leaves, which in some cases remain a fresh green and in others assume pink, purple or red tints in winter. Low-growing perennials usually around 1 ft (30 cm) high, they carpet the ground by means of creeping rhizomes and are invaluable for shady areas. They flourish in all except waterlogged or very light soils. As a bonus to the bold evergreen foliage, they have dense heads of purple, mauve or pink flowers on red stems in March or April. Among those which can be recommended are *B. cordifolia* 'Purpurea'; *B. crassifolia*; *B.* 'Abendglut', 'Ballawley', 'Silberlicht' and 'Sunningdale'.

Helleborus

For brightening up the garden in winter and early spring, there are few plants to surpass the hellebores. Most of them actively prefer shade and are not particular about the soil, as long as it is not too dry. None grow more than 2 ft (60 cm) tall. The Lenten roses, *H. orientalis* and its progeny, are probably the best known, with nodding bowl-shaped flowers of cream, white, purple, pink or crimson, often spotted inside and flushed with green. Another deciduous hellebore, *H. atrorubens*, has unusual plum-purple blooms with yellow anthers and is a lovely sight in late January. The evergreen *H. corsicus* is notable for the prickly blue-green foliage, forming a background to pale green, pendent cups. The native stinking hellebore, *H. foetidus*, is also worth growing, with its clump of deeply divided, dark green, evergreen leaves and bell-shaped flowers of light green edged with purple.

Hosta

Hostas are superb foliage plants for furnishing shady parts where the soil does not dry out. They look equally impressive in a natural woodland setting, in a formal border, or edging a patio in a town garden, and their usefulness is now appreciated by many gardeners. The leaves, in gradually spreading clumps, provide a striking architectural feature throughout late spring and summer and often again in autumn; they are supplemented by spikes of trumpet- or bell-shaped flowers in the summer. The average height of these robust perennials is $1\frac{1}{2}$–$2\frac{1}{2}$ ft (45–75 cm). Unfortunately the foliage is enticing to slugs, which should be kept at bay with slug pellets, and rabbits can also cause damage.

The most widely available hostas include *H. crispula* – dark green, long, pointed leaves with broad, wavy, white margins and pale lilac flowers in June; *H. fortunei* 'Albopicta' – a flower arranger's favourite, having distinctive, pale yellowish foliage bordered with light green in May, maturing to soft green, and lavender flowers in July and August; *H. lancifolia* – shiny, dark green, narrow leaves and deep lilac blooms in September; *H. sieboldiana* var. *elegans* – huge blue-grey leaves, turning yellow in autumn, and dense lilac-white flowers in summer; *H.* 'Thomas Hogg' – similar to *H. crispula*, but larger leaves, with wider, creamy white edging, and pale mauve flowers; and *H. ventricosa* – a large grower, with glossy, rich green, heart-shaped foliage and lovely, deep violet blooms in July and August.

Paeonia

Although the herbaceous peonies are often thought of as sun-loving plants, some can be grown successfully in shade. They do well on chalk or any other kind of soil, so long as it is fertile and well drained. A notable example is *P. emodi*, which prefers shady conditions and grows about 3 ft (90 cm) high. Beautiful, pure white, fragrant flowers, with golden anthers, appear on arching stems in late spring and the smooth, dark green leaves prolong the interest through the summer. The old-fashioned double red peony, *P. officinalis* 'Rubra Plena', also gives full value in shade. Some 1½–2 ft (45–60 cm) high, it blooms in May and the foliage remains attractive until autumn (see p.98). (See also p.96 for shrubby peonies.)

Phlox

The numerous border phloxes descended from *P. paniculata* are tall plants to 4 ft (1.2 m) or more, with heavy pyramids of scented flowers at their peak in August. These come in a range of brilliant and softer colours, which are apt to burn in full sun. Phloxes are therefore better planted in a shady bed and require rich, not too dry soil.

A NORTH-FACING WALL OR FENCE

A wall or fence facing north may seem a daunting prospect to the gardener. However, by careful selection of plants, it can be transformed into an unusual feature and several climbers and wall shrubs are seen to advantage in such a situation. Fruits such as morello cherries, red and black currants, blackberries and loganberries also give good results when trained against a northerly wall. (For further details, see *The Fruit Garden Displayed*.)

Concerning the type of shade and other conditions, much the same remarks apply as for a north-facing border (see p.94). A number of shrubs are suitable for both positions, either free-standing in a border or supported by a wall or fence – for instance, chaenomeles, garrya and pyracantha. Most of those mentioned below are equally successful in an east-facing aspect, which could be described as part shade, receiving sun in the mornings only. The major caveat to this is the camellia, whose blooms will be injured if they thaw too quickly after frost. An alternative use for many of the true climbers, like *Hydrangea petiolaris* and honeysuckle, is to allow them to clamber into the branches of deciduous trees (see p.128). With especially vigorous ones, this is often more satisfactory than a wall, where they tend to grow to the top and leave the lower part bare. (For further suggestions, see *Choisya, Hedera.*)

Once again, thorough preparation of the soil is essential and particularly so near a wall, where the earth is often dry and impoverished.

Shrubs

Berberidopsis

The coral plant, *B. corallina*, is an evergreen climber to about 15 ft (4.5 m) high and 8 ft (2.5 m) wide, with dark green, spine-edged leaves. From July to September it is bedecked in gorgeous, deep red, globe-shaped flowers crowded in hanging clusters. A native of Chile, it is not completely hardy and should be given the protection of a wall, where it is sheltered both from strong sun and from cold drying winds. It requires a deep moist soil and dislikes limy conditions.

Camellia

Many camellias thrive in a north-facing position (see also p.94) and some of those with a more open habit are particularly suitable for training against a wall. Among *C. japonica* cultivars which may be singled out for the purpose are 'Lady Clare' – spreading, almost pendulous, with large semi-double rose-pink flowers; and 'Nagasaki' – vigorous, with semi-double carmine blooms spotted white. Of the *C. × williamsii* hybrids, there are 'Elegant Beauty' – arching, with deep rose, anemone-form flowers; and the outstanding 'J. C. Williams' – horizontal growth, with a profusion of single phlox-pink blooms. Perhaps the best of all, however, is 'Francie L.', an allied hybrid, which has large, semi-double, deep rose flowers and long dark leaves.

Chaenomeles

Familiarly known as "japonica", the various forms of *C. speciosa* are perfect for the small garden, happy in sun or shade, against a wall or in the open. Much-branched, spreading, deciduous shrubs, they are generally some 6 ft (1.8 m) tall and slightly less in width. They flower continuously from February or March to June and sometimes again in autumn, although blooming less freely in shade. 'Cardinalis' is an old cultivar with crimson-scarlet flowers, while 'Moerloosii' (sometimes incorrectly called 'Apple Blossom') has large white flowers suffused with pink and carmine; the dwarfer 'Simonii' has deep red semi-double blooms. The hybrids of *C. speciosa* grouped under the name *C. × superba* are lower-growing, mostly 3–4 ft (90 cm–1.2 m) high, and just as attractive. There is a choice of glowing colours, from the deep red with golden anthers of 'Crimson and Gold', to the orange-scarlet of 'Knap Hill Scarlet' and the brilliant crimson of 'Rowallane'.

Clematis

The numerous species and hybrids of clematis are deservedly among our most popular climbing shrubs. Although they revel in full sunshine, a surprising number of them will succeed against a north- or east-facing wall and all like to have their roots in shade. In many cases they preserve their colour better out of the sun. A good choice can be had from the hybrids which flower in spring and early summer, such as the well-known 'Bees' Jubilee' – blooms of mauve-pink with deep carmine bars; 'H. F. Young' – abundant, large, wedgwood-blue flowers with cream stamens; and 'Nelly Moser' – an old favourite, with huge, flat, pale pink blooms striped carmine (see p.105). Some of the later-flowering hybrids can also be tried, for instance, 'Comtesse de Bouchaud' – satiny rose blooms with cream stamens; 'Hagley Hybrid' – delicate shell-pink flowers; and the stalwart 'Jackmanii' – masses of purple flowers with green stamens.

Cotoneaster

The familiar *C. horizontalis* is an indispensable shrub for a north- or east-facing wall, making a neat herringbone pattern of branches up to 10 ft (3 m) high, thickly covered with tiny leaves. These turn rich orange and red in autumn, creating a pleasant picture with the abundant bright red berries, and do not fall until the new year. It may also be grown in the open, as a low spreading shrub, or used to cover a bank.

Chaenomeles × *superba* 'Knap Hill Scarlet' bears a profusion of flowers in spring and early summer

Euonymus

The versatile *E. fortunei* var. *radicans* is a creeping or trailing evergreen shrub, rooting at intervals from the long stems as they cover the ground or climb up a wall, where it may grow to a height of 20 ft (6 m) or more. The leaves are oval and dark green or, in the attractive form 'Variegatus', greyish green margined with white and occasionally tinged pink. It tolerates deep shade and succeeds in town gardens.

Garrya

A bushy shrub some 6–12 ft (1.8–3.5 m) high and as wide, G. elliptica is a fine evergreen for planting against a wall or fence or on its own. It appreciates a sheltered sunny spot with rather dry soil, but can be grown in shade. Male plants are more ornamental, having long, silvery grey catkins in winter.

Hydrangea

The climbing hydrangea, H. petiolaris, is invaluable for clothing large expanses of a north-facing wall and for growing into tall trees. It may also be used to cover old tree stumps. Clinging by means of aerial roots, it reaches a height of 50–70 ft (15–21 m) and produces a mass of flat flower heads in summer, consisting of small greenish white florets in the centre and larger white florets at the edges. It is deciduous.

Jasminum

The rambling angular branches of the winter jasmine, J. nudiflorum, are best supported by a wall or fence and, although it likes sun, it does not mind the shade of buildings. It grows 12–15 ft (3.5–4.5) high and is always a welcome sight in winter, when the starry, bright yellow flowers appear on leafless green stems. The long growths should be cut back immediately after flowering. It is also excellent planted at the top of a steep bank and allowed to hang down it.

Parthenocissus

A tendril-climbing vine 20–30 ft (6–9 m) tall, P. henryana is happiest grown against a north-facing wall, where the markings of the deciduous foliage are most apparent. The dark green or bronze leaves develop a silvery variegation on the veins before turning red in autumn.

Pyracantha

The firethorns or pyracanthas are undemanding evergreen shrubs, which may be planted in the open or, for greatest effect, against a wall. The one most frequently seen on house walls, P. coccinea 'Lalandei', has a height of 12–15 ft (3.5–4.5 m) and spread of 10–12 ft (3–3.5 m), with white hawthorn-like blossom in June, followed by orange-red berries in autumn and winter. The taller P. atalantioides is distinguished by its larger, dark green,

Left: The flowers of Clematis 'Nelly Moser' do not become bleached in shade

Right: 'Danse du Feu', the popular climbing rose, may be grown on a wall or trained to a support

shining leaves and long-lasting scarlet fruits throughout the winter. More compact plants 8–10 ft (2.5–3 m) high are the thorny P. rogersiana, with small dainty leaves, lovely white flowers and plentiful reddish orange berries; and P. 'Watereri', which is very prolific in bright red fruits.

Rosa

Roses are essentially sun-loving and many gardeners might despair of being able to grow them in shade. However, there are a number of roses, mainly climbers, which have proved their worth in a north-facing situation.

The well-known 'Danse du Feu', one of the first of the modern repeat-flowering climbing roses, bears orange-scarlet double flowers throughout the summer and grows to around 12 ft (3.5 m). 'Maigold' lives up to its name with a display of very fragrant, bronze and yellow, semi-double blooms in May and sometimes flowers again in late summer. It is thorny, but has fine glossy foliage and may be grown either as a climber, to some 10 ft (3 m), or as a shrub, making a mounded bush 5 ft (1.5 m) high (see p.81). Another recurrent-flowering climber, 'Parkdirektor Riggers' produces blood-red semi-double flowers in abundance over a long period. It has dark green, shining leaves and reaches a height of 12–15 ft (3.5–4.5 m). The vigorous 'Hamburger Phoenix' also has a long season of bloom, from June onwards, with crimson semi-double flowers. The velvety, scarlet-black, scented, double flowers of 'Guinée' make an unusual contribution at the same time. On the other hand, 'Soldier Boy' flowers mainly at mid-summer, with clusters of single scarlet-crimson blooms. Like most of the repeat-flowering climbers of restrained growth, it may be trained as a pillar rose and grown in a border if no wall space is available.

Many of the older roses have still not been superseded, although some have the disadvantage of only one flush of bloom. Dating from the early nineteenth century, 'Félicité Perpétue' is a strong rambler to 10 ft (3 m), with semi-evergreen leaves and rounded, fully double, creamy white flowers in July. It is excellent for clambering into an old fruit tree. The noisettes, a group of roses with clusters of distinctively perfumed flowers, were developed during the same period and named after their raiser. One of the few to survive is 'Madame Alfred Carrière', more akin to a modern climber in its ability to flower continuously from mid-summer into autumn. A rampant grower which may attain 20 ft (6 m), it is ideal for covering a large wall and bears sweetly fragrant, whitish, pink-flushed, double flowers. The noisettes were later crossed with the tea-scented roses, the resulting hybrids combining the vigour and hardiness of the first with the colouring and scent of the second. A fine example of a climbing tea-noisette and a favourite of the Victorians, 'Gloire de Dijon' is richly perfumed and seldom out of flower after midsummer. The flat double blooms open buff and change to apricot and pink. Unfortunately only once-flowering, 'Madame Gregoire Staechelin' is equally vigorous and smothers itself in large, loose, double, rose-pink blooms, heavily scented, in June. Similarly, 'Paul's Lemon Pillar' gives a single burst of flower in June, with large, shapely, double blooms, of pale yellow fading to white, set off by large green leaves. 'Climbing Madame Caroline Testout', a climbing variety of an old hybrid tea rose, is more restrained at 8–10 ft (2.5–3 m) high, and very thorny, with double, warm pink flowers at mid-summer, usually repeated in autumn.

Fragrant double flowers of an intense dark crimson in summer and autumn are the hallmark of 'Grüss an Teplitz'. This distinctive rose has strong arching shoots, 6–8 ft (1.8–2.5 m) high, and may be treated as a climber or kept as a large shrub by pruning. The hybrid perpetuals, a large class of roses which were very popular with the Victorians, have left us 'Hugh Dickson', with brilliant crimson, double flowers in summer. A lanky grower of great vigour, it is often seen with the long branches pegged down or bent over hoops and it may also be trained as a climber. 'Conrad Ferdinand Meyer', a robust descendant of R. rugosa, is best grown as a climber, otherwise making a gaunt shrub 8–10 ft (12.5–3 m) high. Large, full-petalled, silvery pink flowers, with a heady fragrance, appear in early summer and again in September.

Schizophragma

Closely allied and similar to the climbing hydrangea (p.104) S. hydrangeoides is a vigorous, self-clinging, deciduous climber, 30–40 ft (9–12 m) tall. It has flat heads of yellowish white flowers with heart-shaped yellow bracts in July and may be used in the same way as its relative.

PARTIAL SHADE

As the day progresses and the shadows change position, different parts of the garden become shaded. These will vary considerably according to the season and height of the sun.

Partial shade is the easiest type of shade to deal with, since so many plants appreciate protection from the full strength of the midday sun. The majority of plants already described would succeed, together with those recommended later for dappled shade (pp.113–125). The climbers and wall shrubs suitable for a north-facing wall (see p.100) are equally good on an east-facing one, with the important exception of camellias and rhododendrons, whose flowers might be harmed by the combination of frost and early morning sun, leading to rapid thawing. A westerly aspect offers particularly favourable conditions, as it is normally warm, sheltered and well supplied with moisture, and here the choice of plants is endless. A west-facing wall broadens the scope even further, offering shelter to many desirable shrubs which might otherwise be regarded as tender.

The list below is therefore confined to a selection of herbaceous perennials and annuals (given in that order) for a partially shady bed or border. For further recommendations, see Anemone, Bergenia, Hosta, Phlox (pp.97–100).

Perennials

Actaea

The baneberry, A. rubra, makes a good companion plant in the shade of shrubs and prefers a cool, fairly moist situation. Poisonous but attractive red berries are borne on spikes 1–1½ ft

The bugbane, *Cimicifuga racemosa*, does not need staking despite its height

(30–45 cm) long in early autumn, above green fern-like leaves. A very similar species, *A. spicata*, is distinguished by the glistening black fruits.

Alchemilla

With its lovely, greyish green leaves and delicate sprays of pale yellow flowers in early summer, *A. mollis* or lady's mantle enhances any mixed planting. About 1 ft (30 cm) high, it is amenable to sun or shade and spreads rapidly from self-sown seed. The flower heads can be cut off before the seeds ripen to keep it within bounds. It succeeds in town gardens and is beautiful in flower arrangements.

Aquilegia

The aquilegia long-spurred hybrids look particularly effective when massed among shrubs or herbaceous plants. They grow to about 2 ft (60 cm) and have attractive bluish grey foliage, with the columbine flowers in a great range of colours appearing in June and July. They seed themselves freely, but are best renewed regularly from bought seed, in order to preserve quality (see p.84).

Astrantia

The commonest species, *A. major*, is 1–2 ft (30–60 cm) high, with clumps of lobed leaves. In summer and autumn it produces unusual star-like flower heads, composed of greenish pink florets with a collar of bracts. It appreciates a moist soil.

Campanula

The cool blues, purples and whites of the bellflowers always seem appropriate in a shady border or woodland setting and they bring a breath of fresh air to town gardens. Some of them can be dangerously invasive, for instance *C. rapunculoides*, which spreads both by roots and by seed and should be avoided. However, *C. latifolia* is more easily controlled and makes clumps of rounded leaves, with 4 ft (1.2 m) stems carrying long funnel-shaped blue flowers in July; there is also a white form. Useful for its smaller stature is *C. glomerata* var. *dahurica*, which is some 1½ ft (45 cm) high and has wide violet-purple blooms.

Cimicifuga

The bugbane, *C. racemosa*, is an elegant border plant where the soil is sufficiently moist. Emerging from ferny foliage, the wand-like stalks reach 5–6 ft (1.5–1.8 m) and are topped with fluffy racemes of white flowers in July.

Dicentra

Known by various names such as bleeding heart, Dutchman's breeches and lady's locket, *D. spectabilis* is an old favourite in gardens. About 2 ft (60 cm) high, the gracefully arching stems are hung with rosy crimson heart-shaped buds opening in late spring, while the bluish green, finely cut leaves prolong the interest. It thrives in a position which is shaded during the hottest part of the day and does well in town gardens.

Gentiana

The willow gentian, *G. asclepiadea*, is a reliable plant for almost any situation and soil, although doing best in cool moist conditions. The arching stems, to 2ft (60 cm) high, are clad in willow-

Geranium himalayense, a beautiful example of the versatile cranesbills

like leaves and bear narrow bell-shaped flowers of rich blue in late summer.

Geranium

The cranesbills, members of the large genus *Geranium*, are among the most valuable hardy perennials, easily grown in all types of soil and often developing into dense groundcover. They can be recommended for town gardens. Many are tolerant of shade and some prefer it. To the first category belong *G. endressi* and its cultivars – vigorous clump-formers 1½ ft (45 cm) or more high, with handsome foliage and pink flowers continuously in summer; the slightly smaller *G. himalayense* (*G. grandiflorum*) – blue-purple veined blooms in July; and *G. × magnificum* – prolific violet-blue flowers in early summer.

In the second category, of definite shade-lovers, are *G. macrorrhizum* – an excellent carpeting plant about 1 ft (30 cm) high, with aromatic leaves and magenta, pink or white flowers according to the form, from May to July; mourning widow, *G. phaeum* – remarkable, very dark maroon flowers, varying to grey or white, in late spring, and the closely related *G. punctatum*; and *G. nodosum* – some 1½ ft (45 cm) high, with hummocks of glossy leaves and lilac flowers from spring into autumn, happy even in dry deep shade.

Viola

Many members of this extensive genus prefer cool shady conditions and a moist but well-drained soil. The vigorous *V. cornuta* forms clumps of small, rich green leaves and bears a profusion of lilac-purple, pale mauve or white flowers in spring. If these are then cut over, it will give a second crop in autumn. The hybrid *V.* 'Huntercombe Purple' has similar requirements, with large, deep purple blooms in spring and summer. Succeeding in dense shade or sun, *V. labradorica* is a scentless violet with purple-flushed foliage and lavender-blue flowers. It runs freely underground and can be a nuisance (see p.133). (See also p.112 for pansies).

Annuals

Asperula

The annual woodruff, *A. orientalis*, is a hardy annual no more than 1 ft (30 cm) tall, with fragrant, pale blue, tubular flowers in summer. It may be sown outside from March to May and will perform well in a shady bed or border.

Begonia

Some of the most popular and versatile summer bedding plants are the wax begonias derived from *B. semperflorens*. Of bushy habit and usually under 1 ft (30 cm) high, they come in a variety of colours and often have bronze or purple leaves. They need warmth to raise from seed, but are widely available as plants from garden centres.

Collinsia

A hardy annual for a moist shady spot, *C. heterophylla* (*C. bicolor*) attains a height of 2 ft (60 cm) and produces two-lipped blooms of white and lilac or purple from June to September. It should be sown in the open in March or April.

Cynoglossum

The hound's tongue, *C. amabile*, is a biennial which succeeds when treated as an annual, sown in March and April. Growing

111

1½–2 ft (45–60 cm), it has grey-green leaves and turquoise-blue flowers in summer.

Digitalis

The wild foxglove, *D. purpurea*, has been largely replaced in gardens by cultivars with white, pink or apricot flowers. Stately plants some 4 ft (1.2 m) high, they are normally biennial and easily raised from seed sown in spring. They will grow almost anywhere, but look most at home in informal surroundings.

Impatiens

A hardy annual to 6½ ft (2 m) tall, *I. glandulifera* bears clusters of long purple flowers in early autumn. It self-sows freely and has become naturalized in parts of Britain.

The numerous busy lizzies, descended from *I. walleriana*, are usually grown as half-hardy annuals and will bloom all through the summer in sun or shade.

Lobelia

The many named forms of *L. erinus*, with flowers of violet or white as well as deep blue, are indispensable edging plants. They are generally sown under glass in February, for planting out in May.

Nemophila

Baby blue eyes, *N. menziesii*, is a hardy annual about 6 in. (15 cm) high, with feathery foliage and charming sky-blue flowers with white centres from June onwards.

Nicotiana

Various species of *Nicotiana* have contributed to the evolution of the modern tobacco plants, in a range of colours from crimson and mauve to lime-green and white. In some, the trumpet-shaped blooms open at dusk and are powerfully scented, in others the flowers remain open by day but are less fragrant. They vary in height from 3 ft (90 cm) to 1½ ft (45 cm). Seed may be sown under glass as late as April and all will be content in a shady position.

Viola

Pansies grown as half-hardy annuals, from seed sown in spring to flower in the summer, are a delightful addition to a shady border. There are many different colours from which to choose.

DAPPLED SHADE

Dappled shade is produced by deciduous trees whose height, shape and type of leaf allow sunshine to filter through the canopy – for example, ash, silver birch, larch, paperbark maple and rowan. Many plants enjoy these conditions, in which they experience continuous light shade during the summer and are never in direct sun. The one serious snag is that they are deprived of much of the moisture and food essential to their welfare by the roots of the trees. Birch has such hungry roots that, even if one attempts to improve the soil for the sake of the plants beneath, the tree itself will probably benefit most.

Despite these disadvantages, dappled shade gives scope for varied and interesting planting at all levels, from shrubs to perennials and bulbs. A large number of plants, including rhododendrons, lilies and primulas, appreciate the broken light provided by trees and associate well to create an impression of natural woodland. In addition to these, most of the plants already recommended are worth trying in dappled shade and some, for instance, hellebores, lilies of the valley, aquilegias, campanulas and ferns, are particularly appropriate in an informal setting.

Lilies, like the lovely yellow *Lilium szovitsianum*, revel in dappled shade

Shrubs

Arctostaphylos

The bearberry, *A. uva-ursi*, is a prostrate trailing evergreen and covers the ground with masses of dark green foliage, sometimes becoming purplish in winter. Tiny white or pink urn-shaped flowers appear in April, giving way to red berries. Together with the very similar *A. nevadensis*, it prefers a lime-free soil and is a useful carpet under rhododendrons and other shrubs. It is also good for clothing dry shady banks.

Camellia

Camellias (see p.94) lend themselves to a natural woodland site, where the canopy is high and the shade not too dense. They are excellent with rhododendrons and share their soil requirements.

Daphne

The spurge laurel, *D. laureola*, is a bushy shrub up to 4 ft (1.2 m) high, with shining, dark, evergreen leaves and rather insignificant, yellowish green blossom in early spring. The slightly taller *D. pontica* produces a profusion of fragrant flowers in April. Both are useful woodlanders, liking a moist peaty soil.

Gaultheria

The creeping wintergreen, *G. procumbens*, is an attractive evergreen carpeter 2–6 in. (5–15 cm) high, with tufts of shining, dark green leaves and white bell-shaped flowers in summer, followed by bright red fruits. It is ideal for covering the ground beneath shrubs. The more rampant salal, *G. shallon*, forms thickets about 4 ft (1.2 m) high and across. It has tough, leathery, evergreen leaves and clusters of pinkish white flowers giving way to dark purple fruits. Its invasive tendency may be controlled by cutting back in early spring. Gaultherias are best in moist lime-free soils containing peat or leafmould, but will tolerate dry conditions.

Linnaea

The twinflower, *L. borealis*, is a diminutive, mat-forming, evergreen shrub, with pinkish white funnel-shaped flowers in summer. The variety *americana* is stronger and more satisfactory in gardens. It needs lime-free soil, but does not object if this is dry.

Mahonia

One of the finest of all evergreen shrubs, M. *japonica* grows some 7 ft (2 m) high and bears long drooping clusters of fragrant yellow flowers from winter to early spring, against a background of large, glossy, deep green, pinnate leaves. The hybrid M. 'Charity', flowering in November and December, is in the same class, but has upright or spreading flowers of a more intense yellow. Both flourish in quite heavy shade beneath trees, their foliage making an impressive foil for other plants, and are happy on all soils.

Rhododendron

The vast genus *Rhododendron* numbers hundreds of species and thousands of hybrids, the majority of which – in particular the well-known large-leaved kinds – are woodland plants par excellence. A high tree canopy not only supplies the cool shady conditions they prefer; it also helps to give protection against late frosts, which might kill the flowers, and to provide shelter from drying winds. However, all rhododendrons are moisture-lovers and surface-rooting and will not withstand competition from greedy trees like beech, birch or sycamore. For this reason, thin oak woodland is often recommended as the best place for rhododendrons, since the roots of the oaks are deep enough not to compete, while their leaves admit sufficient light. An acid soil (preferably pH 5) is essential, with peat and leafmould incorporated, and it should be moist but well drained. The following is just a small selection of some of the most dependable species and hybrids, all of them evergreen.

A dense shrub some 8 ft (2.5 m) high and 5 ft (1.5 m) across, R. *bureavii* has a coating of rusty red hairs on the undersurface of the leaves, with silvery young growths and rose-pink flowers in April and May. Slightly larger, yet bushy and compact, R. *wardii* produces saucer-shaped yellow blooms in May, thus escaping any risk of frost damage; it is important to choose a good form of this variable species. Growing as tall as 20 ft (6 m), R. *rex* has huge leaves, grey underneath, and large trusses of pink flowers in April and May. It succeeds in cold districts. The earlier flowering R. *fulvum*, about 15 ft (4.5 m) high, opens its pale pink blooms in March. The foliage is a polished dark green, with orange-brown felt beneath. The diminutive R. *ciliatum*, 4 ft (1.2 m) in height and spread, also flowers in March, with bell-shaped bluish pink blooms, and benefits from overhead protection.

One of the most famous hybrids, Naomi grows to about 15 ft (4.5 m) and has large clusters of fragrant, yellow-tinged, lilac flowers in May. There are several fine clones such as 'Exbury

Naomi'. Of similar height and exceptionally vigorous and free-flowering, 'Loderi King George' bears large, scented, pink to white blooms in May. It is a definite woodlander, needing shelter and shade. Also best in shade, since the flowers tend to burn in open sunshine, is 'Mrs G. W. Leak'. It grows to some 10 ft (3 m) and has widely funnel-shaped flowers, pink with a dark eye. Another medium-sized plant, Vanessa carries soft pink flowers in June, while the clone 'Vanessa Pastel' had cream pink-flushed blooms. The 12 ft (3.5 m) high Azor is valuable for its late flowering, in June and July, the trumpet-shaped blooms being salmon pink. For the small garden, few can compete with Elizabeth, a delightful spreading shrub only 5 ft (1.5 m) tall, with blood-red flowers in April. Finally, the evergreen azalea 'John Cairns', less than 3 ft (90 cm) in height, has dark orange-red flowers in May.

Stranvaesia

Although it is a rather gaunt-looking shrub or small tree, 20–30 ft (6–9 m) tall, S. davidiana is a valuable screening plant for a shady spot. It is a handsome sight in autumn, when some of the dark green leaves turn bright red and the branches are hung with bunches of brilliant crimson fruits.

Vaccinium

The native cowberry, V. vitis-idaea, is an excellent underplanting for rhododendrons and shares their soil and cultivation requirements. A low carpeting shrub, it forms neat tufts of evergreen box-like foliage, developing bronze tints in winter. The pinkish bell-shaped flowers in early summer are succeeded by dark red berries. It tolerates dry soil.

Xanthorhiza

An interesting deciduous shrub 2–3 ft (60–90 cm) high, the yellow-root, X. simplicissima, is valued mainly for the handsome divided and lobed leaves on erect stems. These turn bronzy purple in autumn and panicles of tiny purple flowers are borne in March and April. It spreads freely by suckers in any reasonable soil, but dislikes chalk.

Opposite above: The well-known Elizabeth, a small growing rhododendron with large flowers

Below: Xanthorhiza simplicissima is an uncommon but striking foliage shrub

Perennials

Ajuga

In the wild, the bugle, *A. reptans*, is found in woodland glades and clearings, carpeting the ground with small, oval, evergreen leaves and, in early summer, with blue flowers on upright shoots. There are several coloured-leaved forms, such as 'Atropurpurea' – purple foliage; 'Multicolor' – bronze, pink and yellow; and 'Variegata' – grey-green and cream (see p.120). It prefers a moist position.

Arisarum

The mouse plant, *A. proboscideum*, makes an interesting ground-cover for dappled shade and a fairly moist soil. Among the shiny green spear-shaped leaves are hidden whitish flowers, with long protruding tails like those of mice. The foliage dies down by July (see p.120).

Aruncus

The goat's beard, *A. dioicus (A. sylvester, Spiraea aruncus)* is a superb herbaceous plant up to 5 ft (1.5 m) in height, with decorative fern-like leaves and great feathery plumes of creamy white blossom in June. The cultivar 'Kneiffei' is a miniature version with finely cut leaves. They are often recommended for a moist spot, but are content with any soil, in shade or sun (see p.83).

Athyrium

The lady fern, *A. felix-femina*, flourishes in shade and, although best in moist humus-rich soil, it will put up with dry conditions. The light green, lacy fronds unfold in late spring and reach some 2 ft (60 cm) high, before dying back in September. It sows itself readily.

Blechnum

The native hard fern, *B. spicant*, is an excellent plant for moist woodland, where it forms increasing clumps of glossy, dark green fronds, above which rise taller, slender, fertile fronds 1–1½ ft (30–45 cm) high. It is evergreen and will tolerate dry soil so long as this is lime-free.

Brunnera

A good strong-growing groundcover some 1½ ft (45 cm) high,

Winter aconites and *Cyclamen coum* are a charming combination in
early spring

B. macrophylla has large heart-shaped leaves and blue forget-me-
not flowers from April to June. The foliage, particularly in the
form 'Variegata', is apt to scorch unless the plant is given a
sheltered shady situation in a moisture-retentive soil.

Cornus

The creeping dogwood, *C. canadensis* (*Chamaepericlymenum
canadense*) is a semi-herbaceous plant some 6 in. (15 cm) high,
with underground shoots which rapidly colonize the ground.
Lovely white flowers, consisting of four bracts, appear in May
and June and the leaves turn reddish purple in autumn. It is happy
in acid, fairly moist, woodland conditions.

Cyclamen

A great favourite for massing under trees, *C. hederifolium*
produces its dainty pink, white or mauve flowers at a most
welcome time of year, from September to November. In addition,
the foliage remains attractive throughout the winter – a deep
green with lovely silver mottling. This is probably the easiest
species to grow, in any type of soil, and spreads from self-sown
seed. It has the remarkable advantage that it will thrive even in the

Above: *Ajuga reptans* 'Variegata' (left), a useful variegated bugle for groundcover; the mouse plant, *Arisarum proboscideum* (right), always fascinates children

Below: *Lamium maculatum* and its form 'Beacon Silver', in front, which also succeeds in shade

deep shade of yew or cedar. The dwarfer *C. coum*, some 3 in. (7.5 cm) high, is another amenable species, with carmine flowers from January to March and dark red undersurfaces to the leaves (see p.119).

Dicentra

Succeeding in a cool shady position, *D. formosa* produces 1½ ft (45 cm) stems with locket-like pink or red flowers in May and June, dangling above delicate ferny leaves. It spreads by means of suckers. The popular 'Bountiful' has deep mauve-pink flowers.

Epimedium

Valued chiefly for their foliage effect, these perennials have the bonus of charming spurred flowers on airy stems in spring. All about 1 ft (30 cm) high, they gently colonize the ground once established and are perfectly happy even in dry shade. Perhaps the most attractive is the evergreen *E. perralderianum*, with bright green spiny-edged leaves, turning coppery bronze in autumn, and yellow flowers. The red-tinged leaves of *E. × rubrum* later become orange and yellow and the flowers are crimson. Flowering in May, *E. × versicolor* 'Sulphureum' has yellow blooms and copper-tinted foliage. All are good in town gardens.

Galax

A low-growing plant, forming hummocks of rounded, shiny, dark green leaves, *G. aphylla* (*G. urceolata*) sends up spikes of white flowers in summer. The evergreen foliage is bronzy in winter. It does best in dappled shade in lime-free soil.

Galium

The sweet woodruff, *G. odoratum*, is better known as *Asperula odorata*. Only 4–6 in. (10–15 cm) high, it rapidly develops into dense drifts of whorled foliage, with heads of scented, pure white flowers from May to July.

Lamium

A fast and efficient colonizer where the soil is sufficiently moist and cool, *L. maculatum* has dark green leaves with a white stripe and flowers of magenta, pink or white. It can be recommended for town gardens.

Lilium

It is not surprising that such an extensive genus as *Lilium* should contain both sun- and shade-lovers. While many demand as much sun as possible, some prefer light overhead shade, or partial shade, especially during the hottest part of the day. Others, for instance *L. martagon* and *L. pardalinum*, are quite adaptable to full sun or shade. The one prerequisite for all is perfect drainage and the majority do best on lime-free soil with leafmould or peat added.

In fact, most lilies appreciate coolness and shade at the roots and shelter from wind. They grow well in company with shrubs or herbaceous plants and seem more at home in natural surroundings, where they can spread freely, than in a formal flowerbed. Ideal for growing up through shrubs is *L. auratum*, 4–8 ft (1.2–2.5 m) tall and bearing huge bowl-shaped flowers, white with a golden ray and deep purple spots. However, because of its late flowering, in August and September, it is less successful in the north, unless grown in a pot. Of similar height but blooming slightly earlier, *L. superbum* is a good woodland species, with recurved orange flowers, deepening to crimson at the base and maroon-spotted. The martagon lily, *L. martagon*, has become naturalized in Britain and thrives in ordinary soils, including limy ones. About 4 ft (1.2 m) high, it has whorled leaves and Turk's cap flowers of purplish red spotted with dark purple, in June and July; there is a fine white variety. Also useful on limy soils is *L. henryi*, 5–8 ft (1.5–2.5 m) in height, whose arching stems carry apricot-yellow flowers in August. These tend to fade if grown in full sun, as do the orange-yellow blooms of *L. hansonii*, which is 3–5 ft (90 cm–1.5 m) tall. In the same height range, the tiger lily, *L. lancifolium* (*L. tigrinum*), produces bright orange-red, heavily spotted, recurved flowers in August and September; the variety *splendens* is later flowering. The 4–7 ft (1.2–2 m) tall panther lily, *L. pardalinum*, succeeds in very moist soil, having orange-red flowers spotted with purple in July. The unusual Caucasian lily, *L. szovitsianum*, is suitable for both limy and peaty soils. The somewhat bell-shaped flowers, canary-yellow with black spots and brown anthers, appear in June (see p.113).

Liriope

Worth a place in the shade, although of thinner growth there and less floriferous, *L. muscari* makes clumps of broad grassy leaves. The violet-blue flowers, on stiff spikes about 1 ft (30 cm) high, open in August and resemble grape hyacinths. It is equally good as groundcover or for edging a path.

Maianthemum

The neatly carpeting M. bifolium is so named because of the paired leaves, like small lily-of-the-valley leaves. Heads of tiny white flowers appear in May. It makes a thin drift, appreciating cool peaty soil.

Oxalis

A dainty woodland carpeter, 'Rosea' is a soft pink form of the wood sorrel, O. acetosella. Flowering in spring, it is about 4 in. (10 cm) high and has pale green, clover-like leaves. It increases rapidly from self-sown seed (see p.78).

Podophyllum

The May apple, P. peltatum, is an unusual plant for a moist shady site. Some 1 ft (30 cm) tall, the large lobed leaves push up through the ground in spring, followed by white flowers in June and often by red fruits. The slightly taller P. hexandrum (P. emodi) has blush-pink cup-shaped blooms and large, shiny red fruits. Both spread slowly from the fleshy roots (see p.124).

Polygonum

Although many of the knotweeds are too invasive to consider for the garden, P. affine is an excellent ground-covering plant for cool moist soil. The narrow, deep green leaves turn vivid bronze-red in winter and spikes of rosy red flowers appear in autumn. The cultivar 'Darjeeling Red' has richer-coloured flowers.

Primula

A large number of primulas enjoy dappled shade and lend themselves to a woodland atmosphere, mingling well with other plants like lilies and trillium. However, they must have permanently moist, deep soil and many do best in wet conditions, by the banks of a stream or even in a bog (see p.128).

The common primrose, P. vulgaris, is a delightful edging plant for woodland, where the soil is moist and heavy, and increases itself freely. The beautiful sub-species sibthorpii, with masses of lilac-pink flowers in March, is easily propagated by division after flowering. Also suitable for such a position is P. juliae, a mat-like creeping plant with wine-red purplish flowers in April. It is usually represented in cultivation by stronger-growing hybrids, such as 'Wanda', with claret-coloured blooms, and the soft pink 'Garryarde Guinevere' (see p.125).

Left: The curious *Podophyllum hexandrum* is a natural woodlander

Right: The flowers of *Pulmonaria angustifolia* are pink in bud, opening to blue

---

The popular polyanthus comes in a wide range of colours, including blue, yellow, red, pink and white. It is usually raised from seed and flowers over many weeks in spring.

Pulmonaria

Active shade-lovers and valuable for their clump-forming habit, the lungworts are easily grown in any cool moist soil. The old spotted dog or soldiers and sailors, *P. officinalis*, grows to some 1 ft (30 cm) and has heart-shaped white-spotted leaves, usually lasting through the winter, and pretty nodding flowers, which open pink and then turn blue, in spring. Very similar but often considered superior are *P. saccharata* and its forms. The smaller *P. angustifolia*, with long, narrow, dark green leaves and sprays of pure blue flowers, thrives even in dense shade. The earliest to flower, starting in February, is the evergreen *P. rubra*, with coral-red bells.

Tellima

Forming attractive clumps of bright green, rounded or heart-shaped leaves, *T. grandiflora* carries small creamy bells on 2 ft (60 cm) stems from April to June. It is easily grown in the cool shadow of trees or tall shrubs and is happy in town gardens.

Left: 'Wanda', a very free-flowering hybrid of *Primula juliae*

Right: *Trillium grandiflorum* is the commonest of the wood lilies

Tiarella

The foam flower, *T. cordifolia*, is an excellent, low, carpeting plant for cool leafy soil, with rich green, maple-like foliage, bronze-tinted in autumn, and numerous feathery spikes of creamy white flowers in May and June. The taller *T. wherryi*, about 9 in. (22 cm), has light green ivy-shaped leaves and is less spreading in growth.

Trillium

The wake robin, *T. grandiflorum*, is very effective when planted in woodland or among shrubs, provided the soil is moist. It grows 1–1½ ft (30–45 cm) high and has stalkless leaves in threes and three-petalled flowers, white becoming flushed with pink in April and May.

Vancouveria

Similar to *Epimedium* (p.121), *V. hexandra* is a useful ground-covering plant some 1 ft (30 cm) high, with small, nodding, umbrella-shaped, white flowers in spring, above elegant, divided, soft green leaves. It is ideal for town gardens and accepts dry soil.

SHADE UNDER TREES

Patches of shade cast by individual trees are a frequent problem. Depending on the density of shade, however, it should be possible to grow the majority of plants recommended for permanent shade (pp.85–94) in these difficult dry conditions. One exception is *Choisya ternata*, which does not appreciate overhanging branches. It is also worth experimenting with some of the plants mentioned under dappled shade (pp.113–125), for example, *Gaultheria shallon*, *Tellima*, *Cyclamen* and *Primula*. Further suggestions are made below.

Bulbs and other spring-flowering plants offer another solution, since they come into growth early in the season before the tree canopy has formed. Wild snowdrops, are ideal for naturalizing under trees, together with winter aconites (see p.119) and early crocuses like *C. tommasinianus*, followed by bluebells.

Shrubs

Juniperus

The vigorous *J. × media* 'Pfitzeriana' will grow even under a cedar tree and is also excellent on a steep slope or bank. The spreading arching branches reach 6–8 ft (1.8–2.5 m) high and across and carry feathery, blue, juvenile leaves among the darker adult foliage. Like all junipers, it tolerates chalky soil.

Perennials

Anemone

As its name implies, the wood anemone, *A. nemorosa*, is well pleased with a situation among or directly beneath deciduous trees and will quickly multiply, especially on heavy soils. The native species bears dainty flowers, white flushed pink, on 6–8 in. (15–20 cm) stems in March and April. There are named forms like 'Robinsoniana', with lavender-blue blooms. Another small anemone, *A. apennina* usually flowers slightly later, in sky-blue. Forms with white or pink and with double flowers also occur. Even the beautiful Japanese anemone, *A. × hybrida* (see p.97), can make a contribution in early autumn.

Lamium

Yellow archangel, *L. galeobdolon* 'Variegatum', (*Galeobdolon luteum* 'Variegatum', *G. argentatum*) is one of the most effective

Anemone apennina makes a carpet of dainty leaves and flowers

groundcovers under trees or large shrubs. Some 1 ft (30 cm) high, it becomes a carpet of dark green and white-marbled foliage and produces yellow dead-nettle flowers in late spring. It is extremely vigorous and likely to smother smaller plants.

Luzula

The rampageous woodrush, *L. maxima* (*L. sylvatica*), is a grass 1–3 ft (30–90 cm) tall, with broad, green, tufted leaves and pale brown flowers. It should always be used with discretion, because of its greedy roots, but is invaluable for larger areas under trees and for steep banks and other awkward sites.

Polygonatum

Adaptable and easily grown, Solomon's seal, *P. multiflorum*, has long arching stems to 3 ft (90 cm), clad with attractive shiny leaves and, in May and June, hung with numerous whitish green bells. It and its commoner hybrid, *P. × hybridum*, delight in cool woodland, but will grow in almost any sort of shade.

Smilacina

The false spikenard, *S. racemosa*, is related to Solomon's seal and closely resembles it apart from the small open flowers, which are carried in a creamy white, scented spray at the end of the stem.

MOIST SHADE

Moisture and shade provide a perfect combination for many plants. A number of those already described prefer to be grown in soil which never dries out,including *Brunnera macrophylla*, *Cimicifuga racemosa*, *Gentiana asclepiadea*, *Podophyllum*, *Polygonum affine* and *Pulmonaria*. *Ajuga reptans* and *Aruncus dioicus* do best in damp, even boggy conditions.

Several ferns revel in a moist shady position, among them *Matteucia struthiopteris*, *Onoclea sensibilis* and *Osmunda regalis*. Eye-catching foliage plants for the waterside are *Rodgersia aesculifolia* and the smaller *R. pinnata* 'Superba'. The vast genus *Primula* contains many true moisture-lovers, such as *P. denticulata*, *P. florindae*, *P. alpicola* and *P. japonica* cultivars. (For details, see the Wisley Handbook, *Water Gardens*.)

CLIMBERS FOR TRAINING INTO TREES

In the wild, many climbing shrubs use deciduous trees for support, with their roots and lower stems in shade and their flowering parts emerging through the branches into sunlight. This idea can easily be adapted for the garden and adds another dimension of interest, particularly where space is limited.

Once again, however, the help given by the tree in providing support is partially offset by competition from its roots. One way round this is to dig a large hole and place a bottomless wooden box in it, fill it with good soil and then plant the climber in it. The box will eventually rot, by which time the climber should be well established. This precaution is not necessary if the tree is old or if the climber has aerial roots, for example *Hydrangea* and *Schizophragma* (p.104 and p.107). The planting hole should be made at least 3–4 ft (90 cm–1.2 m) from the base of the trunk, which will also reduce competition from the roots. The climber can be trained into the tree along a bamboo cane, pole or wires, tying it loosely if required. Most climbers will do no harm to their hosts, but it would obviously be unwise to choose a very strong-growing plant like a vine for a small apple tree.

Many of these climbers also make excellent groundcover for difficult places, but must be kept within bounds and prevented from smothering other plants.

Above: The cultivars of *Primula japonica* are ideal for moist shade

Below: *Clematis montana* (left), a familiar sight in May and June with its profusion of blossom;
Lonicera japonica 'Halliana' (right), a rampant evergreen honeysuckle

Suitable climbers include *Actinidia chinensis, Akebia trifoliata, Clematis montana, Lonicera japonica* 'Halliana', *L. tragophylla, Rosa filipes* 'Kiftsgate' and *R. helenae* (see p.129). (For details, see the Wisley Handbook, *Climbing and Wall Plants*.)

ALPINES AND DWARF PLANTS FOR SHADE

Raised beds and sinks or troughs offer a convenient modern alternative to the rock garden, particularly where space is lacking, and the presence of shade need not be a deterrent. A number of dwarf plants tolerate or actually prefer shade, including *Campanula portenschlagiana, Chiastophyllum oppositifolium, Erinus alpinus* 'Mrs Boyle' and 'Dr Hanaele', *Hacquetia epipactis, Omphalodes cappadocica, Primula auricula* and *P. marginata* forms and *Ramonda myconi*. (For details, see the Wisley Handbook, *Alpines the Easy Way*).

Some plants can also be grown in crevices on the shady side of a stone or brick retaining wall – round a terrace or raised bed perhaps. Ferns like *Asplenium ruta-muraria, A. trichomanes, Ceterach officinarum* and *Polypodium vulgare* are particularly useful.

Sharply drained soil is a prerequisite for alpines. However, in a shaded sink, raised bed or wall, where the rain rarely penetrates, conditions tend to be excessively dry. They can be improved by incorporating organic matter, which helps to retain moisture.

Spring-flowering dwarf bulbs are also good in a raised bed or trough, although they may look less attractive when they have finished flowering and the leaves are dying down (see p.132 for suggestions). For further recommendations, see *Anemone, Athyrium, Blechnum, Cyclamen, Tiarella, Viola*.

Left: The pink-flowered *Erinus alpinus* is excellent for a shady wall

Right: *Hacquetia epipactis*, a valuable shade-loving alpine

Left: The superb *Omphalodes cappadocica* flourishes in partial shade

Right: Shade is essential to the lovely *Ramonda myconi*

CONTAINERS IN SHADE

Shade in the garden often goes hand in hand with poor or dry soil, as well as a shortage of space, and here containers have distinct advantages, since the essential elements – growing medium, drainage, watering – are all under control. A loam-based compost, such as John Innes No. 3, is best for shrubs and trees in large containers, while one of the proprietary peat-based composts would suit smaller plants. Both types normally contain an adequate supply of fertilizer. Free drainage can be ensured by making holes in the base of the container (if they are not already there) and then putting a layer of broken flower pots, pieces of brick or stones in the bottom, before filling up with compost. Watering is a matter of judgement and, although containers will dry out less quickly in the shade than in sun, they may not receive much rain from above.

Because the most important factors are taken care of, containers allow a wider range of plants to be grown in shade than might otherwise be possible. A permanent feature can be made of shrubs and perennials, while bulbs, bedding plants and annuals can be used at will. The short-term plants are particularly valuable for achieving quick results and contributing a splash of colour where it is most wanted. (See also the Wisley Handbook, *Gardening in Ornamental Containers*.)

Plants recommended for containers in shade are as follows:

Shrubs

Aucuba japonica (p.86)
Buxus sempervirens (p.86)
Camellia japonica (pp.94–5)
C. × williamsii (pp.94–5)
Choisya ternata (p.86)
Clematis (p.102)
Euonymus fortunei var.
  radicans (p.103)
× Fatshedera lizei (pp.86–7)
Fatsia (p.88)
Hedera helix (p.88)
Ilex aquifolium (p.88)
Prunus laurocerasus (p.89)
P. lusitanica (p.96)
Rhododendron (pp.115–17)
Rosa (pp.105–7)
Taxus baccata (pp.90–91)
Vinca major (p.91)
V. minor (p.91)

Perennials

Bergenia (p.99)
Hosta (pp.99–100)
Lilium (especially L. auratum)
  (p.122)

Annuals (pp.111–13)

Asperula orientalis
Begonia semperflorens
Impatiens (busy lizzie)
Lobelia erinus
Nicotiana (tobacco plant)
Primula (polyanthus)
Viola (pansy)

Spring-flowering bulbs are excellent and easy plants for containers in shade, always welcome for their early display. Dwarf kinds are best, especially in a window box or round the base of a shrub in a large container. The choice could include crocuses, chionodoxas, scillas and grape hyacinths; daffodils, for instance, Narcissus cyclamineus and its cultivars; irises such as Iris reticulata; and tulip species like Tulipa fosteriana and T. greigii and their hybrids.

Bulbs which are slow to establish, notably snowdrops, winter aconites, snowflakes (Leucojum vernum) and Anemone blanda are better given a permanent home in a raised bed or trough (see p.130).

Finally, a mention for one of the finest of all container plants, the fuchsia. These beautiful tender shrubs flower almost as well in shade as in sun, continuing for several months in summer and autumn. Among the numerous cultivars are neat bushy forms for pots and window boxes, cascading types for hanging baskets and others for training into standards or pyramids.

Opposite: Viola labradorica, an invasive but pretty violet for a shady spot

Foliage Plants

— URSULA BUCHAN —

Evergreen foliage can be clipped into shapes: box spirals, golden privet domes and yew balls and pyramids decorate this garden

Introduction

Everyone knows that the word "foliage" is the collective name for the leaves of a plant or tree, but many are less certain about what is meant by "foliage plant". This is hardly surprising, considering there is no precise definition. Many plants have interesting, unusual or beautiful leaves, but they also flower, of course. The hosta, for example, is usually referred to as a foliage plant, yet it has pretty and quite conspicuous flowers. *Fatsia japonica* is another plant with striking flowers which one would nevertheless label a foliage plant. The most useful definition of the words "foliage plant" which I can think to offer you is – a plant grown at least as much, and usually more, for its leaves as for its flowers. Fortunately, although it is necessary for me to be logical about what I include in this section, the gardener seeking to plant up his or her garden does not need to know exactly where to draw the line.

Even a moment's reflection on the subject makes one realize how many and various are foliage plants and how much they can enhance the beauty of gardens. For one thing, evergreens and evergreys (as silver-leaved sub-shrubs like artemisias are sometimes called) give colour to an otherwise brown and twiggy garden scene in winter and provide a useful solidity in summer. Deciduous foliage plants have a far longer season of interest than even such seemingly perpetual flowerers as the potentillas and there is, in many cases, the added bonus of a change of leaf colour in autumn.

Densely packed leaves, whether deciduous or evergreen, are important, and sometimes vital, as a background. Foliage is the perfect foil to colourful flowers, yet it can create its own substantial visual impact as well. Even shrubs which we do not consider primarily as foliage plants have flowers too small to be seen from a distance, so that it is their leaves which supply the initial impression. By providing an apt contrast, bold leaves serve to emphasize the airiness of many flowers.

Such is the range of plants which we can honestly call foliage plants, and such the range of uses they can be put to, that I have resolved to limit myself, arbitrarily but understandably, to hardy, or almost hardy, plants and to those which you have at least a sporting chance of finding in a local nursery or garden centre. I

Opposite: The striking blue-grey leaves of *Hosta tokudama*, which grows to about 1½ ft (45 cm) high and wide

have arranged them in what I consider the most useful way, namely by leaf colour. However, I do appreciate that the distinctions are sometimes a little blurred, as in the case of *Acaena* 'Blue Haze', which, in the preparation of this section, has see-sawed between the grey and the blue chapters! In each chapter the plants are listed alphabetically by their botanical names, in groups, beginning with evergreen trees and ending with perennials, biennials and annuals. That seems to me the most logical way of proceeding if this section is to be any help at all in the vexed and highly complicated area of garden design. So important do I consider this subject that the first chapter is specifically concerned with the uses of foliage plants and with how felicitous plant groupings may be achieved with them. I stress the words 'plant groupings' because I think that whole borders composed, artificially and self-consciously, only of foliage plants are a mistake; without the contrast of flower shape and colour, the garden changes too subtly and slowly for me, at least, fully to appreciate it.

I have described plants which I consider to be particularly good foliage plants. After all, of those on sale, some are decidedly better than others. As the choice is a personal one, it is possible that some readers' favourites may have been omitted, for which I am sorry.

I have not given details of cultivation, since the requirements of foliage plants are just like those of other plants. However, it is worth mentioning that some foliage shrubs and trees may be encouraged to produce leaves twice as big as usual, by pruning them in a particular way and then feeding them with well-rotted manure or compost. The purple-leaved hazel, *Corylus maxima* 'Purpurea', the coloured-leaved forms of elder, *Sambucus*, the purple smoke bush, *Cotinus coggygria* 'Royal Purple', *Eucalyptus gunnii* and the variegated varieties of *Cornus alba* all respond well if their stems are cut back to within 1 ft (30 cm) of the ground in March. This stooling, as it is called, also ensures that the shrubs do not produce flowers or fruits which would detract from the foliage. When carried out on eucalyptus, the plant retains its more attractive, bluer, juvenile foliage. Poplars and catalpas can also be pollarded, by cutting back the tree trunk to within a few feet of the ground. This will lead to the formation of a crown of young branches to give a good foliage effect. (See also the Wisley Handbook, *Pruning Ornamental Shrubs*.)

Opposite: 'Royal Purple', a form with dark purple foliage of the smoke bush, *Cotinus coggygria*

Uses and Associations of Foliage Plants

It is all very well collecting together a disparate assortment of attractive plants which you would like to see growing in your garden but, if there is no thought as to their placing and particularly their interrelationship, the result will be a formless muddle, sometimes accidentally effective, it is true, but always haphazard and chancy. Those plants which we grow as much, if not more, for their foliage as for their flowers can play many important roles – in unifying plant groupings; defining boundaries; acting as long-lasting recurring themes, focal points and foils; and providing contrasts and harmonies of leaf colour or leaf shape. It is even possible for them to combine more than one of these functions.

Evergreen foliage plants provide an unchanging (or subtly changing, in the case of some conifers) unifying theme in the garden all year. While the hectic flow of colour is supplied by flowers, the evergreens remain a constant, if understated, device for preserving the scheme from the threat of garishness. You only have to think of grass to realize how successful a massed foliage plant can be for setting off bright displays of flowers. Evergreen hedges made of yew and Lawson cypress act as a solid background to define more sharply what is growing in front, as well as to provide shelter. Evergreen climbers like *Clematis armandii* give year-round contrast of colour against a brick or stone wall.

Plants with bold ascending leaves, such as yucca, phormium, iris, sisyrinchium and ornamental grasses, make excellent focal points or accent plants for the ends of borders or beside entrances. The effect is usually heightened, rather than undermined, when the vertical flower stems emerge.

Other good focal points can be established by using plants with very bold or large leaves, like rodgersia, rheum, gunnera, acanthus, globe artichoke and fatsia, whose foliage will draw the eye. These plants should not be overworked, of course, or their impact will be diminished. How much they should be used depends on the size of the border and cannot be dogmatically computed.

One of the most important functions of foliage plants in garden schemes is to provide contrasts of shape and texture which the eye will willingly accommodate. In this respect, far more is possible than with variously coloured flowers, which easily tire the eye with jarring contrasts. Among many possible combinations of

A successful example of foliage associations, with *Rheum palmatum rubrum* providing the emphasis at The Dower House, Boughton House, Kettering

---

foliage one might take as examples palmate rodgersia next to pinnate ferns (p.152), or the huge leaves of *Rheum palmatum rubrum* with euphorbias and ferny-leaved dicentra (above). Some feathery foliage, particularly that of conifers, is close-set and therefore looks dense, whereas the leaves of ferns are widely spaced and lighter in atmosphere.

It must never be underestimated how vital is the foliage plant's contribution to colour in the garden, nor how effective even simple associations can be. However timid you may be about colour schemes, you can scarcely go wrong massing a collection of grey-leaved plants, for instance, because, even though the foliage differs, there are only subtle gradations of leaf colour. I have to say, however, that a whole border of this kind can seem a little dull on an overcast day and I prefer small groupings. The varying colours of hostas also harmonize beautifully together, making this one of the most successful foliage plants for summer (provided slugs are kept at bay).

Plants with two-colour variegations, particularly cream and green, lighten the appearance of a border and make the planting look less dense when set close to those with uniformly coloured leaves. Gold-variegated plants create a slightly warmer and more sumptuous effect than cream- or white-variegated ones. Those plants which grow in shade or semi-shade (the golden variegated hostas immediately spring to mind) are especially useful,because gold-leaved plants often lose their brightness in shade. Curiously, combinations of gold- and white-variegated plants tend to detract from rather than enhance each other. Plants with similar variegations but different leaf shapes, such as *Hosta crispula* next to *Euonymus* 'Emerald Gaiety', work well together. Of course, such agreeable harmonies lose their force if overdone.

Variegated plants with three or four colours in the leaf, for example, *Ajuga reptans* 'Multicolor', are not easy to place; in general terms, it is safest to take account of whichever is the dominant colour from a distance and include them in a scheme which requires that colour.

The use of coloured-leaved trees is much more acceptable in a garden context than in the landscape but, because of sheer mass, it is wise to group a striking tree like *Robinia pseudacacia* 'Frisia' with green-leaved trees of different foliage form or texture, or to place it on its own; next to purple *Acer palmatum* forma *atropurpureum*, for example, the effect is a little crude. In the case of coloured-foliage trees, both evergreen and deciduous, restraint is sometimes necessary: a mixture of brightly coloured dwarf conifers can be restless in their variety. Cream and green variegations can be added to a scheme if the purple is too heavy, as it can be in late summer. Thus, the variegated *Cornus alba* 'Elegantissima' would lighten the effect of *Acer platanoides* 'Crimson King', for instance, or *Prunus* × *cistena*.

Red, purple or pink leaves are pleasantly set off by glaucous or grey foliage. Combinations such as *Festuca glauca* and purple berberis or *Cotinus coggygria* 'Royal Purple' and *Pyrus salicifolia* 'Pendula' work well. Purple sage makes a good contrast for any grey foliage plant. Green leaves will also complement grey: *Alchemilla mollis* looks well with grey carpets and its lime-green flowers are not startling enough to be offensive. The effect can be made more complex and satisfying by contributing bronze and

Ruta graveolens 'Jackman's Blue', purple sage, *Helichrysum italicum,*
Euphorbia characias and *Senecio bicolor* ssp. *cineraria* give a good
mixture of leaf shapes and colours

blue-grey in the shape of *Foeniculum vulgare purpureum* and
Acaena 'Blue Haze'.

The unusual brown and black tints of *Sedum* 'Vera Jameson'
and *Ophiopogon planiscapus nigrescens* can be grouped with the
grey-blue of *Euphorbia myrsinites* or the yellow of *Carex oshimen-
sis* 'Evergold'. The splendid yellow form of the meadowsweet, *Filipendula ulmaria* 'Aurea', can be happily planted next to
the glaucous *Hosta sieboldiana* var. *elegans* or the silver and green
Pulmonaria saccharata 'Argentea'. These would be fine companions too for *Sambucus racemosa* 'Plumosa Aurea'.

Purple and yellow are often matched because they are comple-
mentary colours, but the combination can be over-used. The first
instance of it in a garden is startling and effective, the second is
already a slightly irritating cliché. Most commonly seen is a
mixture of purple-leaved berberis with the yellow-leaved *Philadelphus coronarius* 'Aureus', which works quite well even when
the berberis turns red in autumn.

It is possible, particularly if the gradations are not too abrupt, to make successful groupings with many different colours or, more precisely, shades of colour. It is also rare for differing shades of autumn colour to jar.

Small foliage plants, like flowers, are best planted in groups or swathes, lines or curves, in fact anything but singletons or dots. Large-leaved plants like fatsia, on the other hand, can make an impact on their own. Whatever is done should be done boldly, simply and unfussily. My personal preference is for groupings which travel diagonally towards the back of the borders rather than merely edge the bed.

It is neither necessary nor desirable to devote a garden entirely to foliage plants. Flowers are valuable for contributing seasonal interest and diversity of form, as well as for attracting wildlife. The same colour considerations apply when combining foliage plants with flowers, although it is as well to remember that flowers are often fleeting and that the dominant association may still be between the leaves of the plants concerned, regardless of how showy the flowers are.

EXAMPLES OF PLANT ASSOCIATIONS

Almost any plant permutation will work within each group below. Some suggested combinations are indicated by the numbers in brackets – i.e. all those with (1) would go together.

For a sunny border

Actinidia kolomikta (on wall) (1)
Artemisia absinthium 'Lambrook Silver' (1)
Ballota pseudodictamnus (1)
Fuchsia magellanica 'Versicolor' (1)
Helictotrichon sempervirens (1)
Ruta graveolens 'Jackman's Blue' (2)
Salvia officinalis 'Purpurascens' (1/2) and 'Tricolor' (2)
Alchemilla mollis (2)
Stachys byzantium 'Silver Carpet' (2)
Acaena 'Blue Haze' (2)

For damp shade

Hosta tokudama (1)
Ajuga reptans 'Atropurpurea' (1) and 'Multicolor' (1)
Bergenia purpurascens (1)
Euphorbia amygdaloides 'Rubra' (2)
Juniperus squamata 'Chinese Silver' (2) (if shade not too dense)

Hosta ventricosa 'Aureomarginata' (2)
Hedera colchica 'Dentata Variegata' (2)
Athyrium niponicum pictum (1)
Pulmonaria saccharata 'Argentea' (2)
Tellima grandiflora rubra (2)

For the waterside

Gunnera manicata (1)
Filipendula ulmaria 'Aurea' (3)
Iris pseudacorus 'Variegata' (1/2/3)
Lobelia 'Queen Victoria' (1/2)
Glyceria maxima 'Variegata' (1/2)
Milium effusum aureum (3)
Rheum palmatum rubrum (2)
Rodgersia aesculifolia (3)

Leaf textures and variations in green

Fatsia japonica
Juniperus horizontalis 'Emerald Spreader'
Acer palmatum dissectum
Vitis coignetiae (up tree or over wall)

Gold and purple in sun

Corylus maxima 'Purpurea' and *Catalpa bignonioides* 'Aurea'; *Robinia pseudoacacia* 'Frisia', *Cotinus coggygria* 'Royal Purple' and *Cornus alba* 'Spaethii'.

A SELECTION FOR AUTUMN COLOUR

Fraxinus excelsior 'Jaspidea'
Populus × canadensis 'Aurea'
Robinia pseudoacacia 'Frisia'
Ginkgo biloba
Liriodendron tulipifera
Acer palmatum 'Dissectum Atropurpureum'
Berberis × ottawensis 'Superba'
Cotinus coggygria 'Royal Purple'
Hydrangea quercifolia
Vitis coignetiae
Vitis vinifera 'Purpurea'

Green Foliage

As with flowers, one does not grow all foliage plants purely for their colour. Indeed, that is hardly more than half the reason. Closely linked to colour, and often influencing it, is leaf texture and there is the multiplicity of leaf shape to consider as well. The possible combinations of these variable factors is what makes the choice so enormous, so fascinating and, it must be said, sometimes rather daunting.

CONIFERS

All conifers are foliage plants, but some are considerably more interesting than others. The ones with most impact are those with striking forms as well as good foliage. Such a one is Brewer's weeping spruce, *Picea breweriana*. This makes a pyramidal shape, up to 20 ft (6 m) in time, with branches from which grey-green shoots hang down vertically.

The charm of *Chamaecyparis nootkatensis* 'Pendula' lies (like Brewer's spruce) in the fact that the branchlets hang down from the horizontal branches creating, in a well-grown specimen, a curtain of dark green foliage. This is a conifer which will grow to about 33 ft (10 m) or more high and is tolerant of an exposed cold position.

Juniperus horizontalis 'Emerald Spreader' is a completely prostrate juniper, with bright green foliage. It can spread up to 6 ft (2 m). Junipers have the advantage of being perfectly content in alkaline soils.

Ginkgo biloba is the maidenhair tree, the only living representative of an ancient order of plants. It is not the easiest plant to establish, but worth the effort, for it makes a beautiful, broadly columnar tree in time. It is a deciduous conifer and the unique (in a tree) fan-shaped leaves, partially divided in the middle, turn a buttery yellow in autumn. It is tolerant of chalk, but will need a warm sunny place if it is to do well. The best known tree in this country, although not the tallest, is the old specimen near the Orangery in the Royal Botanic Gardens, Kew, which was planted in 1762.

Opposite: *Acer palmatum* var. *dissectum* should have a sheltered sunny position if it is to thrive

DECIDUOUS TREES

Acer palmatum var. *dissectum* is a very slow-growing maple, which makes a round-headed shrub rather than a tree. The palmate leaves are finely cut, with up to 11 lobes, which are themselves deeply divided and toothed. The leaves turn red or yellow in autumn. (See p.146.)

Fagus sylvatica 'Aspleniifolia', the fern-leaved beech, makes a lovely tree in time, reaching more than 50 ft (15 m) high and with a wide canopy. The leaves are not uniform: some are long and narrow, others very deeply cut.

Liriodendron tulipifera is another tree with odd-shaped attractive leaves. They are mid-green, smooth, have four lobes and are cut almost square at the end. This is the tulip tree, but it does not produce its goblet-shaped, yellow-green and orange flowers until quite mature. The leaves turn yellow before falling. It is not a tree for a small garden, nor indeed for any garden north of the Midlands.

I have included *Sorbus thibetica* 'John Mitchell' for its leaves in spring; they are up to 6 in. (15 cm) long and wide, green above, silver underneath, and they open from the vertical, giving the tree the appearance from a distance of a flowering magnolia. This is one of the whitebeam section of rowans; it becomes quite a big tree, 33 ft (10 m), and is reasonably quick-growing.

EVERGREEN SHRUBS

Fatsia japonica is an "architectural" plant with very bold, glossy, dark green, palmate foliage, divided into 7 or 9 "fingers". This is a strong-growing evergreen and makes several stems which rise up, without many branches, to 10 ft (3 m) or more. The flowers are those of the ivy writ large – great white bobbles in November. Fatsias are best grown against a wall in cold districts; they thrive in town gardens because their leaves shrug off atmospheric pollution.

Santolina rosmarinifolia ssp. *rosmarinifolia* is the rather neglected green-leaved relation of the silver cotton lavender so popular with "grey borderers". It is worth growing among its silver-leaved brethren; the button-like yellow flowers go quite well with the vivid green, thread-like foliage, and it makes a neat 20 in. (50 cm) high bush, which can be tidied up with a pair of shears after flowering.

Because its tough leaves make it suitable for planting in city centres, *Viburnum davidii* has a local authority air about it. However, it seems hard to condemn a plant for guilt by association, so I try to look at it with a dispassionate eye. The oval leaves are unusually leathery, with three distinct veins down their

148

Above (left): *Yucca filamentosa* slowly forms clumps of evergreen foliage;
(right) *Aralia elata* does best in milder parts of the country
Below (left): *Vitis coignetiae* may be allowed to clamber into a tree or
cover a stump; (right) the large lobed leaves of *Hydrangea quercifolia*
develop lovely autumn tints

lengths. It makes a low, wide-spreading, dense mound and, if male and female are planted together, will provide bluey turquoise berries on red stems.

Yucca filamentosa has large, lovely, creamy white flowers in 3 ft (1 m) panicles, but it is, nevertheless, usually grown for the sword-shaped, green-glaucous, stiffly pointed leaves. It needs a warm, dry, sunny position and is a little winter-tender. It is well worth the effort of protecting, however, with a thick layer of peat round the base. (See p.149.)

DECIDUOUS SHRUBS

Everyone knows the horse chestnut, with its huge palmate leaves, but few have enough space to plant one. Fortunately, there is a shrubby version, more suitable for the average garden, called *Aesculus parviflora*. It spreads by suckers, so it makes a wide-reaching deciduous thicket. The white flowers, in panicles up to 1 ft (30 cm) long, open in July and August. The leaves colour well in the autumn.

Aralia elata, the Japanese angelica tree, not only has large handsome leaves, but it is also an unusual shape. It is a deciduous suckering shrub, which can grow up to 33 ft (10 m), though usually about 13 ft (4 m). It has few branches and those there are, are spiny. The leaves, which are doubly pinnate, can be more than 3 ft (1 m) long and are held on slightly pendulous branches. This is a fine "architectural" plant for the larger garden. The flowers are great frothy plumes of white in early autumn. (See p.149.)

Hydrangea quercifolia has leaves deeply scalloped like those of the American red oak, *Quercus rubra*, hence its specific name. The stems are woolly and the green leaves turn to red, orange and purple in the autumn. It never grows more than 6 ft (2 m), often much less, and makes a handsome, slightly pendulous, spreading shrub. Like all hydrangeas, it needs to be sited where its terminal buds will not be burned by early morning sun after a frosty night and it does best in a sheltered position. The flowers are borne in white panicles throughout the summer. They are set off very well by the smooth green leaves. (See p.149.)

Vitis coignetiae is a glorious plant. It is a very vigorous climber which will soon, with a little help, scramble up 65 ft (20 m). The leaves are an interesting bold shape, being often 1 ft (30 cm) across, toothed, heart-shaped at the base and with usually three lobes. They are glossy green above, with a thick brown felt beneath. As if that were not enough, the leaves, particularly those in the sun, turn every shade of vermilion, orange and purple-crimson in autumn. (See p.149.)

The unusual dark green foliage of *Helleborus foetidus* contrasts with the flowers

PERENNIALS

No account of foliage plants could ignore *Acanthus spinosus*, considering that the leaves were the inspiration for the pattern on Corinthian columns in ancient Greece. However, the stately purple-hooded flowers gathered round the 3 ft (1 m) stems in July and August are almost equally striking. Be careful when weeding near this plant for the leaves and stems are spiny.

Alchemilla mollis is the darling of the flower arrangers. Its only possible fault is a tendency to seed too widely, for in all other respects it is perfect. The fresh green leaves are pretty, particularly when they have collected raindrops, and it is aptly named 'lady's mantle' because of the neat gathering of their serrated edges. The flowers, up to 20 in. (50 cm) high, are a froth of yellow-green in midsummer. It makes a most agreeable companion to silver and purple foliage plants. The dwarf species, *Alchemilla erythropoda*, is ideal for rock gardens.

Gunnera manicata is exotic in all its parts and particularly in its huge spine-backed leaves, which stand up like umbrellas blown inside out, and grace the edge of many a lake or running stream in large gardens. The leaves have been known, in favourable conditions (that is, wet and warm), to reach 10 ft (3 m) in diameter and most resemble those of a giant rhubarb on long prickly stems. The plant is not very hardy and the crown is best protected by its own leaves laid over it in winter. The flowers are curious rather than

151

Left: The imposing leaves of *Gunnera manicata* make an excellent focal point
Right: The bold palmate foliage of *Rodgersia aesculifolia* is highlighted by the delicacy of ferns

---

beautiful: green cones, some 20 in. (50 cm) in length, appear in spring and gradually turn brown as the season proceeds.

Helleborus foetidus has green bell-shaped flowers and is prized by some for these, but I grow it for the thin "finger" leaves, divided right to the "palm", because it is they which are evident for most of the year. A rare native of British chalk woodlands, it is a very useful plant for a shady place. (See p.151.)

Rodgersia aesculifolia is not easy to find in nurseries and garden centres, but nevertheless worth seeking out if you have need of something large for a moist, preferably peaty, soil. The leaf is similar to that of a horse chestnut, except that it has seven leaflets; it grows up to 10 in. (25 cm) long. The flower spikes are large and white and appear in summer.

FERNS

Few people, even convinced foliage gardeners, think hard enough about growing ferns, despite their being accommodating plants, happy in rather dreary, shady, damp places. Their beauty is subdued and they do not flower, but I love the myriad sorts of our native lady fern, *Athyrium filix-femina*. 'Victoriae' for example, has a criss-cross pattern on the green fronds, which are crested on their margins. Also outstanding is *Matteuccia struthiopteris*, for its bishop's crozier fronds in spring which unfurl into upright arching branches, hence its name shuttlecock fern. These ferns are happiest in woodland conditions.

152

Silver and Grey Foliage

Most, although not all, grey and silver foliage plants originate in hot dry places. That is why they usually have many little hairs on both sides of the leaves, to prevent them losing too much moisture. The use of these plants in garden design must therefore be guided by their need for light well-drained soil and full sun (indeed, the drier and poorer the soil, the whiter the leaves will become). One of the reasons that grey borders have become so popular is that the vast majority of grey- and silver-leaved plants require the same conditions. However, without a leavening of purple-, green- and blue-leaved foliage plants, it is easy to have too much of a good thing. After all, grey-leaved plants can look drab on cloudy days and the sun cannot be guaranteed to shine all summer.

Many of these sun-lovers are members of the daisy family and have yellow, often rather coarse, daisy flowers. The industrious gardener removes these, not only because they are often un-

The grey border in the garden at Abbots Ripton Hall, Huntingdon

interesting and detract from the purity of the plant's greyness, but also because the neat foliage looks tatty, even losing some of its colour, as the plant comes up to flower. Because the greyness or silveriness of these plants results from hairs on green leaves, the appearance can change when rain wets them, so that what was a grey border can look quite green. The leaves also tend to start green in spring, until the hairs have grown. The sophisticated colourist will take all these factors into account.

CONIFERS

There are few conifers which can honestly be said to be grey or silver, rather than blue-grey (see p.169), but one such is *Juniperus squamata* 'Chinese Silver'. The foliage is very silvery, with only a hint of blue. It is a multi-stemmed shrub rather than a tree; the branches point up and out and have pendulous tips. It grows to about 6 ft (2 m) with a spread of 5 ft (1.5 m).

Juniperus 'Grey Owl' has silvery grey foliage and makes a semi-prostrate shrub with a spread of 6 ft (2 m) or so. It is not a dense shrub but has a pleasing airy appearance.

DECIDUOUS TREES

Among the deciduous trees, *Populus alba* stands out because of the effect of the white woolly undersides of the three-lobed leaves as they tremble in the wind. They turn yellow in autumn. This is a tree for the outer limits of a large garden, for it grows to 65 ft (20 m), with a spread of 6 ft (2 m). No poplar should ever be planted close to a house, owing to the wide-spreading roots which can damage foundations and drains.

Pyrus salicifolia 'Pendula' is a very commonly planted, small tree, mainly because it strikes people as a good choice of present for relations celebrating their silver wedding anniversary. The leaves are weeping-willow-like and very silvery, particularly in full sun. The flowers are white pear flowers, but do little to detract from the overall silver appearance.

EVERGREEN SHRUBS

The silver plants *par excellence* are the artemisias. *Artemisia* 'Powis Castle' has finely cut, silky foliage and grows to about 3–4 ft (1–1.2 m). It does not flower much, unlike *Artemisia absinthium* 'Lambrook Silver'. This is, strictly speaking, a herbaceous perennial, but it has a woody base so finds a place here. It gets to about 2½ ft (75 cm) tall and has fine silvery foliage not dis-

Left: Like most other artemisias, A. *schmidtiana* 'Nana' has aromatic leaves
Right: *Convolvulus cneorum* is not completely hardy but may be easily increased by cuttings

similar to 'Powis Castle'. *Artemisia ludoviciana* var. *latiloba* ramps about a bit, being herbaceous and having a rather vigorous root system, but the willow-like uncut leaves, on lax stems, are very silver. It will grow up to 20 in. (50 cm). One of my favourites is the little *Artemisia schmidtiana* 'Nana': it makes small mounds of finely cut, silky foliage.

Atriplex halimus is the shrubby version of the purslane; it thrives by the sea and is silvery grey in all its parts. It can reach 6 ft (2 m) in a favoured position. The leaves are oval and about 2 in. (5 cm) long. It is reasonably hardy.

Ballota pseudodictamnus is another sub-shrub for the sunny well-drained border. It has curving stems, greeny silver and felted, up to 20 in. (50 cm) in length. The leaves are green at first, but soon develop their white appearance and form rosettes at the tips. The July flowers are small, mauve and held in whorls of bracts. This is not a spectacular plant but a valuable one.

Calluna vulgaris 'Silver Queen' is a useful heather, whose mauve flowers do not clash with the silver grey foliage. Callunas are not lime-tolerant.

Convolvulus cneorum wins hearts wherever it is seen. The combination of fine silky leaves and restrained, white, suffused pink, bindweed flowers is wonderful. Unfortunately, it needs protection in harsh winters. In a sheltered spot, which it well deserves, it will grow to 3 ft (1 m) tall and as much across.

Hebe pinguifolia 'Pagei' is one of the most widely planted prostrate shrubs because it is dependable, reasonably hardy for a hebe and useful as groundcover when planted generously. The trailing stems are composed of many grey leaves and star-like white flowers appear in May.

Helichrysum italicum is the curry plant, so-called because of the smell given off by the leaves when crushed. It is not as impressive as some silver shrubs, but its very white needle-like leaves, on upright stems to about 1½ ft (45 cm), do stand out among greens and greys and it looks good even in winter. It has the usual, not very interesting, yellow flowers at the ends of the shoots, which are best clipped off, as the leaves lose their whiteness when the plant is flowering. Like lamb's ears. *Stachys byzantina*, this is an indispensable plant if you have children to amuse. (See p.143.)

Helichrysum splendidum is an even better plant. It is stunning as a low 2 ft (60 cm) hedge, if cut back in April and trimmed in July – a treatment which has the advantage of preventing it flowering and becoming straggly as it is wont to do. The silver-grey leaves are ribbed and have blunt tips. Also to its credit is a much hardier constitution than is normal with helichrysums.

Lavenders are probably grown as much for their flowers as their foliage, but nevertheless deserve a place here. My favourite, *Lavandula angustifolia* 'Hidcote', grows to about 2 ft (60 cm) and as much across and has purple flowers in short spikes above the narrow silver-grey leaves. It makes an excellent informal hedge or edging next to a path.

Lotus hirsutus is grown less often than its charms warrant. The trifoliate leaves are grey and intensely hairy and it has small, pink-tinged, white, pea flowers in clusters at the end of shoots and from the leaf joints. The seed pods are like reddish star-shaped beans. This shrub will reach up to 20 in. (50 cm) high and will only thrive in a light soil and in sun.

Similar in appearance to *Ballota* is *Marrubium cyllenum*, but much less commonly seen. It has pretty, grey-green, velvety leaves which are a subtle foil to silver plants.

Phlomis fruticosa, the Jerusalem sage, is almost too well known, yet despite its charms being a little overrated, it cannot be omitted from this list. It grows, in height and width, to about 4 ft (1.2 m) and has wedge-shaped, grey-green, wrinkled, furry leaves on young grey stems, which become woody in time. The hooded yellow flowers are borne in whorls at the top of the stems in July. Although reasonably hardy, it only thrives in a sunny well-drained place.

Santolina chamaecyparissus, the cotton lavender, is another silver-leaved sub-shrub which gives of its best if trimmed each April to encourage leaf growth and prevent the plant becoming too woody, and if the little yellow flowers are cut off in July to stop the plant becoming straggly. It then makes a mounded bush about

2 ft (60 cm) high and can be used for an informal hedge. The leaves are very short, about 1 in. (2.5 cm), but there are a great many of them so the shrub appears dense. There is a dwarf variety called *nana* (*corsica*), which is only half the height and more compact in habit.

Santolina pinnata subspecies *neapolitana* has longer, up to 3 in. (7.5 cm), thinner leaves and looks better, in my opinion, even though it is not always very silver. The pale yellow flowers are thickly borne, but have an evil smell. It is as well to cut the plant back after flowering to ensure new silvery growths for the winter. It is reasonably hardy and produces whiter foliage and sturdier growth if grown in fairly poor soil.

For a shrub which really does look white, *Senecio bicolor* ssp. *cineraria* 'White Diamond' is as good as any, although it loses the intensity of whiteness a little as the leaves age. The leaf is less deeply cut than in another, also good, selection of the same species, 'Ramparts'. The only disadvantage of this plant, apart from its doubtful hardiness (it is often treated as a bedding plant), is that it can hardly be dissuaded from flowering.

Brachyglottis (*Senecio*) 'Sunshine' is a much undervalued evergreen shrub for a sunny position, presumably because it is so very easy to grow. Apart from a cutback in April, it looks after itself and does not take long to reach 4 ft (1.2 m), with a 3 ft (1 m) spread. It makes a rounded bush, so that two plants can be handsome placed on each side of a path or entrance. The oval leaves are grey-green above and grey-white below. I try to remember to cut off the stems which will carry the slightly coarse, yellow, daisy flowers in summer. It is reasonably hardy.

DECIDUOUS SHRUBS

Elaeagnus angustifolia and *Elaeagnus commutata* are useful silver foliage shrubs, despite being deciduous. The first is the more vigorous and can become a small tree in favourable conditions, whereas the second scarcely exceeds 6 ft (2 m). *Elaeagnus angustifolia* has narrower, more willow-like leaves than *E. commutata*. Both have small fragrant flowers in early summer, followed by small, silvery, oval fruits.

There is a dwarf willow called *Salix lanata* which has dense clusters of oval leaves covered in soft grey hairs, giving it a silvery green appearance. It rarely grows more than 3 ft (1 m) in height or width and is an ideal plant for a rock garden. The leaves are set off well by egg-shaped, golden yellow catkins in late spring. The woolly willow, as it is aptly named, is a rare native of Scotland, as well as northern Europe and Asia.

Edible as well as decorative, the globe artichoke may grow up to 6 ft (2 m) high

PERENNIALS

(*Artemisia* see pp.154–5.)

Cynara cardunculus is the cardoon. It used to be much prized as a vegetable, but the stems and young leaves require blanching and few people bother any more. However, it does make a striking impact as an ornamental in the large flower border because of its huge, jagged, arching, widespread clump of silvery grey, thistle leaves. The stems of the flowers need staking and are best removed unless you wish to use the blue thistles as dried flowers. The globe artichoke, *Cynara scolymus*, is similar though less silver, and the "globes" must be punctually harvested if the leaves are not to lose their lustre. Both will grow in heavy soils.

One of the more useful rock garden plants, because it will trail on the top of a low wall, is *Euphorbia myrsinites*. It has sessile leaves, which means they have no leaf stalks. The colour of the trailing stems is just the blue side of being strictly grey. The flowers are lime-green and typically spurge-like, but they do not make a great splash.

The silver-leaved deadnettle, *Lamium maculatum* 'Beacon Silver', is a desirable, low, groundcover plant for a semi-shaded

158

Left: *Lamium maculatum* 'Beacon Silver', a valuable silver-leaved plant for a shady spot
Right: *Sedum spathulifolium* 'Cape Blanco' spreads happily in any dry sunny place

position, even if it does seed itself around somewhat. The leaves are smaller than the ordinary green deadnettle and, apart from a thin green margin, almost completely covered in silver-white. Rather attractive pink blotches appear on them in cold weather; these are actually caused by a disease and may reduce growth slightly. Most lamiums (like the true 'Chequers', for example) should be treated with great suspicion because of their invasive habit, but 'Beacon Silver' is relatively innocuous and certainly pretty. The pink flowers do not detract from its appearance.

Pulmonaria saccharata 'Argentea' is a very good form of this white-blotched lungwort and the oval leaves are almost completely covered with silver. It is doubly welcome for being one of the few silver-foliage plants which positively relishes shady conditions. The blue and pink flowers are produced in March. A mulch of shredded bark compost put down in spring is necessary to ensure the required moist conditions throughout the growing season.

Raoulia australis is made up of tiny rosettes of oval leaves which seem to flow through a rock bed like a river of molten silver. It needs full sun, but is generally quite hardy, provided the winter is not too wet or the soil heavy. It has minute yellow flowers in April and May. The whole plant is no more than 1 in. (2.5 cm) high.

The neat, succulent, grey-white rosettes of the ground-hugging rock plant, *Sedum spathulifolium* 'Cape Blanco' (often wrongly called 'Cappa Blanca'), contrast quite agreeably with the yellow flowers in June and July. This is an easy plant for a sunny spot in

The handsome *Salvia argentea* prefers full sun and a dry soil

the rock garden or at the border's edge; it is also very easy to divide and propagate.

Stachys byzantina 'Silver Carpet' is an improvement on the ordinary lamb's ears because the silver quality of the velvety leaves is not undermined by shaggy undistinguished flower spikes. It is an excellent edger for a sunny border.

The best of all silver perennials, in my opinion, is *Tanacetum haradjanii* (*T. densum* 'Amani', *Chrysanthemum haradjanii.*) It is a mat-forming perennial which grows no higher than 6 in. (15 cm) and has leaves so deeply dissected that they look like silver-white feathers. The flowers resemble those of groundsel and should be removed if possible. It is reasonably hardy in a well-drained sunny position.

BIENNIALS

I dislike weeding around the biennial Scotch thistle, *Onopordon acanthium*, because the seedlings are so prickly, but I concede that it is a majestic plant for the back of a big border, even if the erect branching of the winged stems is a bit eccentric. It can reach 8 ft (2.5 m) high and will need staking. The flowers come out in late July; these should be deadheaded if the plant is to retain its silver-grey foliage effect and to prevent it sowing itself everywhere.

Salvia argentea is a most unusual plant, grown not for the mauve-white flowers dotted on the 3 ft (1 m) tall stem in July and

The silver-grey fronds of *Athyrium niponicum* var. *pictum* are most unusual in a fern

August, but rather for the ground-hugging rosette of large, intensely white-woolly, triangular-oval leaves. In a very well-drained sunny spot it may be perennial, but it is more often treated as biennial and seeds quite freely anyway if you can bear to retain the scruffy flower stems.

FERNS

Athyrium niponicum var. *pictum* (*A. nipponicum* 'Metallicum') is a beautiful fern. The green fronds, 8 by 4 in. (20 by 10 cm) are overlaid with silver-grey and contrast well with the deep red stems. It needs a damp humus-rich spot in shade. Once seen, this plant is never forgotten.

— Bronze, Red and Purple Foliage —

The words 'purple-leaved' are much too commonly and loosely applied: plants with leaf colour as various as bronze, pink and deep red frequently have the same epithet *purpureum* tacked on to their names. For example, the bronze-green-leaved form of fennel is *Foeniculum vulgare purpureum*. However, conscious that I may drown if I swim against this particular tide, I have included all the leaf colours in this chapter normally to be found masquerading under the name *purpureum*.

CONIFERS

Microbiota decussata is a first-class prostrate conifer, whose ferny green foliage turns a rich bronze in winter. If planted in groups, it makes excellent groundcover.

DECIDUOUS TREES

Outstanding among deciduous trees is a Japanese maple called *Acer palmatum* forma *atropurpureum*. It has bronzy purple, palmate leaves which turn deep red in autumn. It grows to only about 13 ft (4 m), with a spread of 8 ft (2.5 m), and does best in a slightly acid soil to which humus has been added. Another good form is *Acer palmatum* 'Dissectum Atropurpureum'. This makes a low round-ed bush rather than a tree; it has deep red, very finely divided leaves.

Acer platanoides 'Crimson King' is a cultivar of the Norway maple with glossy, deep purple-crimson leaves, which appear almost black after midsummer. It needs to be placed where the sun will shine on it. It is impressive from a distance but op-pressive close to. Like the other Norway maples, it becomes quite a large tree in time.

The coloured forms of the sycamore are suitable for gardens because, unlike the species itself, they do not become very large. *Acer pseudoplatanus* 'Brilliantissimum' slowly grows into a domed shape and has shrimp-pink new leaves which 'go off' to a dirty green as the summer wears on. A lovely tree to gasp at in other people's gardens.

There are several types of purple beech, hardly distinguishable from each other. The deepest purple is probably *Fagus sylvatica* 'Riversii'. If you want a cut-leaved form, 'Rohanii' is the one to

Acer pseudoplatanus 'Brilliantissimum', a beautifully coloured, small tree, at The Dower House, Boughton House, Kettering

order. These can be used with the ordinary green-leaved common beech to make a 'tapestry' hedge, although all will grow very tall. Beeches like any soil which is not too damp and a sunny position.

I am extremely attached to the hybrid crab apple, *Malus* 'Liset', even though the reddish purple colour of the leaves does not endure but turns to bronzy green as the season wears on. The flowers are deep crimson and the fruits dark red. It makes a round-headed small tree about 20 ft (6 m) tall.

EVERGREEN SHRUBS

Erica carnea 'Vivellii' is a mixture of colours which is just the right side of the vulgar. The foliage is bronze-red and the winter flowers deep carmine. This will not be everybody's choice, but it is an intriguing combination and the winter-flowering heaths have the great advantage of being lime-tolerant.

Phormium tenax 'Purpureum', the purple form of the New Zealand flax, is almost hardy, but needs some protection, such as straw round the base, if you are to be certain of getting it through the winter. It has emphatic sword-like leaves which point sky-wards and sometimes bend over near the tips. It flowers only when it is mature. There is a dwarf form called 'Bronze Baby' which gets to about 1 ft (30 cm). 'Thumbelina' is even smaller. Neither of the latter is very effective when massed; they are better as specimens in the rock garden.

Above: *Pieris* 'Forest Flame' is similar to *P. formosa* var. *forrestii* 'Wakehurst' but of more elegant habit
Below: *Vitis vinifera* 'Purpurea', a highly ornamental grape vine

Pittosporum tenuifolium 'Purpureum' is another rather tender evergreen, or rather, everpurple. The oval leaves on black stems of all pittosporums are distinctive because of their wavy margins and this form adds brown-purple colour as well. The deep purple flowers in spring are inconspicuous but smell deliciously of vanilla. It needs a sunny warm place and, even when suited, seems not to be long-lived.

Salvia officinalis 'Purpurascens' is also a rather short-lived and not especially hardy shrub; nevertheless it is worth bothering about if only because the leaves, like those of all forms of the common sage, can be used as a culinary herb. The leaves are velvety to the touch and of a soft, dusky purple colour which goes so well with grey foliage plants. The purple sage makes a low, slightly mounded bush, about 3 ft (1 m) across, and can be kept tidy by an annual prune in spring. (See p.143.)

DECIDUOUS SHRUBS

Berberis × *ottawensis* 'Superba' is, to my mind, the best of the purple-leaved berberises, although the contest is close. It is a vigorous shrub reaching some 6 ft (2 m) high and across in time, with branches growing upward and arching at the top. The leaves turn a beautiful bright red in autumn before falling. The flowers are yellow and not a major asset to the plant. The berries are red.

Corylus maxima 'Purpurea' has rich purple leaves which also redden in autumn. The coarse and matt leaves of this purple form of the filbert make a good background for finer, lighter leaves. It is a shrub or tree which will attain 16 ft (5 m) in time, unless stooled every two years or so. Interestingly, the catkins and the nuts are also purple.

Cotinus coggygria 'Royal Purple' grows to 8 ft (2.5 m) each way in time and, planted in a sunny place in not too rich soil, will have deep purple leaves which become translucent red in autumn. The common name of this magnificent shrub (or, rather, of the species) is smoke bush, because of the misty masses of tiny purplish pink flowers which it bears in June or July. The combination of colours is very striking. (See p.139.)

Pieris formosa var. *forestii* 'Wakehurst' is for acid soils only, un-fortunately, for this is an eminently desirable shrub. The foliage is brilliant scarlet when young and gradually turns to pink, then white, finally green. Pendulous panicles of white bell flowers are borne in May. It grows to about 6 by 5 ft (2 by 1.5 m). To do well, it should be planted in semi-shade and sheltered from cold winds.

Prunus × *cistena* is the best of the several purple-leaved cherries. The leaves are small, oval and a deep reddish purple; these contrast well with the small but numerous white flowers in March and April. This shrub makes an excellent hedge and should be pruned after flowering. If left to its own devices, it does not grow much above 6 ft (2 m).

Much loved by flower arrangers is the species rose, *Rosa glauca* (*R. rubrifolia*), which can boast grey-purple leaves on reddy purple stems. It is a vigorous shrub which will reach 10 ft (3 m), with a spread of 5 ft (1.5 m). No one grows this rose for its flowers, which are short-lived, small, single and pink, but autumn brings attractive, round, red hips. Seedlings are frequently found nearby. It should be planted in full sun if the leaves are to colour well.

Vitis vinifera 'Purpurea', a form of the common grape vine, colours differently from many purple-leaved shrubs: it starts deep red and becomes purple in autumn. It does produce grapes in hot summers and these, being purple, enhance the imposing effect, but do not taste pleasant. They are definitely not for wine-making. (See p.164).

PERENNIALS

Like all bugles, *Ajuga reptans* 'Rubra' is a thoroughly useful, without being stirring, plant. They make good groundcover in moist, partially shaded places, but will tolerate other conditions as well. This form has reddish purple, glossy leaves which look their best in autumn. The contrast between leaves and deep blue flowers borne in whorls on 4 in. (10 cm) stems in summer is not unpleasing.

Bergenia purpurascens is one of the best of these useful evergreen perennials. The elliptic leaves, which turn inwards and point upwards and so are less good for groundcover than others of the genus, become bright purple-red in winter and are then very ornamental. The magenta flowers are held on 1¼ ft (40 cm) red stems in April and May.

Euphorbia amygdaloides purpurea needs part shade and moist conditions, if it is not to get mildew, and is useless as a single specimen as several are required to make an impact. It is, nevertheless, an interesting plant – worth growing if you have the conditions to please it. The leaves are dark green, suffused with purple; small lime-green flowers are carried on maroon stems in spring.

Foeniculum vulgare 'Purpureum' is at present a vogue plant, for its bluey bronze foliage, so finely cut as to be almost hair-like, is a welcome muted contrast to grey-leaved plants and is edible to boot. A close relative of dill, fennel bears the same yellowish green flowers, but on 5 ft (1.5 m) stems. It is best placed where the sun will shine through it.

The curious dark leaves of *Sedum* 'Vera Jameson' mingle pleasantly with the blue-grey of *Euphorbia myrsinites*

Lobelia 'Queen Victoria' bears little resemblance to the half-hardy lobelia so much used in summer bedding schemes. For one thing, the flower stem grows up to about 3 ft (1 m); for another, it is a short-lived herbaceous perennial. It has vinous purple leaves and stems and scarlet flowers in August and September. It needs protecting with peat as it is not completely hardy.

Ophiopogon planiscapus 'Nigrescens' is a bizarre little plant which looks a bit like tufted grass at first sight. Actually, the colour of the leaves, which is retained all year, is intensely dark purple-brown rather than black, in the same way that so-called "black" hair is really deep brown. The very narrow strap-like leaves get to about 6 in. (15 cm) long and spread out from the tuft almost horizontally. This plant has tiny mauve flowers in August and sometimes black berries in autumn. It must have good moisture-retentive, yet well-drained, soil to thrive. It will increase slowly by its underground stolons.

Rheum palmatum rubrum is the purple-red-leaved form of the ornamental rhubarb and ornamental it is too. It has huge palmate leaves on 3 ft (1 m) stalks, which fade to green after the plant has flowered. The pinky red flowers are produced on 5 ft (1.5 m) long stems in June, followed by striking, brown, flat seed pods. It revels in a moist, humus-rich soil. (See p.141.)

Saxifraga fortunei 'Wada' likes cool, shady, moist conditions where it will make a clump. This is a very good form, with rounded lobed leaves which are a reddish brown-purple on top and crimson-pink below. The white flowers, with their uneven-sized petals, are a good contrast when they come out in October and November.

Sedum 'Vera Jameson' is a most unusual but desirable stone-crop, for the succulent leaves are a curious purple-bronze, bordering on the brown, held on floppy fleshy stems. Flat heads of grey-pink flowers are carried on 1 ft (30 cm) stems in autumn. (See p.167).

Tellima grandiflora rubra is an excellent plant which will grow even in dry shade. The purple-bronze leaves persist all year. It is much better than the ordinary green species, although it has the usual tellima flower spikes of not very exciting, small, greeny yellow bells on 1½ ft (45 cm) stems from April to June.

Trifolium repens 'Purpurascens Quadrifolium' is a four- (or five- or six-) leaf clover with a difference but, one hopes, just as lucky. Its leaves are purple-brown with green margins. Clovers are not difficult to grow (this is a form of white clover, a common weed of lawns), but they appreciate a good moisture-retentive soil. If happy, it will cover the ground well to a height of 4 in. (10 cm). It is another plant to grow if you have children to amuse.

Viola labradorica is a native of Greenland and Labrador, not surprisingly, with small pansy flowers of bluey mauve in late spring. The form *riviniana purpurea* is grown more for the heart-shaped leaves which are a dark greenish purple, especially when young. It comes true from seed and spreads also by underground stems. It seeds itself into crannies in an unvexatious way, looking particularly pretty in the cracks between limestone paving.

ANNUALS

I have included the annual *Atriplex hortensis* var. *atrosanguinea* (*A.h.* var. *cupreata*) because it is deep beetroot purple and also seeds itself about, so need not be renewed every year. It is plain that it is a relative of the weed, fat hen, for it is slightly succulent and has triangular leaves. It grows quickly to 4 ft (1.2 m) and thrives in full sun. The leaves can be eaten like spinach.

Blue Foliage

Those plants which we loosely call 'blue' are, really speaking, blue-grey. They are most usually recognized by the suffix 'Glauca', a word which, like 'Purpurea', embraces a multitude of variation – and wishful thinking. There are few 'blue' foliage plants, just as there are few blue-flowering shrubs. Those that will pass muster are very valuable to the garden designer.

CONIFERS

Abies concolor 'Compacta' is, to my mind, the best dwarf silver fir. It makes a small compact shrub with a dense habit. The foliage is a strong grey-blue, particularly effective in late spring and early summer. It grows very slowly, eventually reaching 3 by 2½ ft (1 m by 75 cm). Firs are not difficult to grow, although they are happiest in acid soils.

Cedrus libani atlantica 'Glauca' is not a tree for small gardens, although it is often to be found in them. It is a lovely, silvery blue in colour, pyramidal in habit, and with branches which sweep to the ground.

Chamaecyparis lawsoniana 'Pembury Blue' is the best known of the blue-grey Lawson cypresses. It is of pyramidal shape and reaches 10–13 ft (3–4 m) by 5 ft (1.5 m) in ten years. It is deservedly popular.

Chamaecyparis pisifera 'Boulevard' is as striking in its way as 'Pembury Blue'. The colour of the soft foliage is intensely silver-blue, particularly in the summer. It never becomes a huge tree, more a conical large shrub. It repays being grown in good, slightly acid soil, in some shade.

There are many 'blue' junipers, all much of a muchness. I think *Juniperus horizontalis* 'Wiltonii' the best; it is a most attractive, completely prostrate shrub, with thin, glaucous, 'whipcord' tips to its long horizontal branches. In ten years it will have spread about 5 ft (1.5 m).

Juniperus scopulorum 'Blue Heaven' is a good cultivar to grow. The foliage is blue and so are the 'berries'. It is closely related to *J. scopulorum* 'Sky Rocket', but of a more intense blue and with a pyramidal rather than columnar habit, growing over 6 ft (2 m) in time. It thrives in full sun. (See p.170.)

Juniperus squamata 'Blue Star', on the other hand, is a dwarf shrub, though with much the same colour of foliage. It is almost prostrate and associates well with heaths and heathers.

There are several kinds of blue *Picea pungens* on the market. As good as any is 'Thomsen', which has strongly silvery blue foliage and an erect habit. It reaches about 25 ft (8 m) in ten years but spreads only 10 ft (3 m).

EVERGREEN SHRUBS

Coronilla valentina ssp. *glauca* is grown as much for the blue-grey pinnate leaves as for the yellow, scented, pea flowers, which come in a flush in early summer and then intermittently throughout the rest of the year in fine weather. It should be grown as a wall shrub in all but the mildest districts and needs occasional trimming for it is naturally a rather floppy shrub.

Eucalyptus gunnii is favoured by flower arrangers for the blue, round, perfoliate (that is, round the stem) juvenile leaves. The 4 in. (10 cm) long, sickle-shaped, adult leaves are not so blue, but this tall tree can be stooled to retain the juvenile leaves. It must have a stake, as it is vulnerable to strong winds.

Hebe pimeleoides 'Quicksilver' is a small, evergreen, spreading shrub, 1¼ ft (40 cm) high, with very good silver-blue leaves on thin dark branches. Small white flowers appear in early summer. It appreciates a sunny place and light soil.

Othonna cheirifolia is not a plant you see very often, although I do not know why. It seems perfectly hardy here in the cold east Midlands, where I grow it over a low wall. It has unique, paddle-shaped, blue-grey leaves on erect young shoots and yellow daisy flowers in June. The whole plant does not get higher than 1 ft (30 cm) and it is not really suitable for massing but, nevertheless, the leaves contrast agreeably with those of other sun-loving foliage plants. (See p.172.)

Ruta graveolens 'Jackman's Blue' is a well-known foliage plant of round bushy habit, with deep blue-grey leaves which are pinnate, up to 5 in. (12 cm) long and rounded at the ends. It is a sun-lover and likes a well-drained soil, but is hardy. It has yellow, not very pleasant-smelling, flowers in summer and it seeds itself about. To maintain a neat bush, it should be trimmed over in April. The foliage has a bitter aroma and can cause a rash if touched with bare hands. (See p.143.)

DECIDUOUS SHRUBS

Berberis temolaica is rarely seen and not easy to find in nurseries. However, despite a rather indeterminate shape, it is worth

Opposite: 'Blue Heaven', one of several blue or silver cultivars of *Juniperus scopulorum*

171

Left: *Othonna cheirifolia*, a low-spreading evergreen shrub from North Africa
Right: Hostas are indispensable foliage plants and *H. sieboldiana* var. *elegans* is among the most eye-catching

growing for its glaucous leaves and purple shoots. In time it will grow to about 6 ft (2 m), but it is slow to establish itself. The flowers are pale yellow, the berries red. It is a striking shrub, particularly in spring when the combination of yellow flowers and blue-grey leaves is very effective.

PERENNIALS

Acaena 'Blue Haze' is a little carpeting plant from New Zealand, with very blue-grey, divided, pinnate leaves and reddy brown burrs. It grows more strongly than the other acaenas and can make quite an impact when planted in a small group. It reaches about 8 in. (20 cm).

Festuca glauca is the well-known blue fescue, a tussock-forming non-spreading grass about 10 in. (25 cm) high. Indeed, one might wish that it were more adventurous. It has very thin, silvery blue, evergreen leaves but, unless massed, it can look a little forlorn.

Helictotrichon sempervirens is another blue grass, this time on a larger scale. It makes a tussock of stiff spiky leaves which grow up to about 3 ft (1 m). The flower heads are yellow and borne on arching stems. It too requires a sunny position in a light soil.

Hosta sieboldiana var. *elegans* has marvellously large, blue-grey, oval, corrugated leaves, as much as 10 in. (25 cm) wide and 1 ft (30 cm) long. These are held on long erect stalks. The flowers are pale mauve, appear just above the leaves and are not exceptional. A similar form is 'Bressingham Blue'. There is also a smaller version, *Hosta tokudama* (see p.136). These hostas do best in a humus-rich soil, in part shade.

172

Gold and Yellow Foliage

A great many plants have a yellow- or golden-foliage form; it is a frequent aberration in the plant world. Our gardens would be much poorer if that were not so, although there are some yellow-leaved plants which simply look ill and give no pleasure. Pretty or not, the fact that the leaves are yellow usually, though not inevitably, means a diminution in vigour because the chlorophyll in the leaf has been masked by another pigment like carotene. The yellow leaves of deciduous plants are often vulnerable to being burned up in bright sunshine, yet few plants colour well in deep shade. 'Reversion' to green leaves is a problem, as it is with variegated plants. Nevertheless, despite these disadvantages in cultivation, yellow-leaved plants are a vital element in the foliage garden, often contributing colour when there is nothing else that will do so. This is particularly true of yellow conifers and I have tried to select forms of conifers, from the masses available, which retain some good colour in winter.

CONIFERS

Chamaecyparis lawsoniana 'Lane' is quite an old variety but is still worth growing, because it does not take up much room, being narrowly columnar in shape. Although it grows in time to 33 ft (10 m) or more, it will only be 6 ft (2 m) wide. It needs a place in full sun.

Chamaecyparis obtusa 'Nana Aurea' is a proper dwarf conifer, for it never grows to more than 2 ft (60 cm) each way and often considerably less. This makes it an ideal candidate for the rock garden or a raised bed in full sun. It becomes a mounded shrub with rounded fans of golden yellow foliage.

Cupressus macrocarpa 'Goldcrest' and 'Donard Gold' are similar; of the two, I marginally prefer 'Goldcrest', which has feathery, reasonably dense, bright yellow foliage. These plants are perfect for southern coastal gardens as they are wind-resistant but not really quite hardy. Neither exceeds 23 ft (7 m) when mature.

Most yellow yews, however garden-worthy, do not keep their colour well in the winter. The exception is a form of the common yew, *Taxus baccata*, with ascending branches, called 'Semper-aurea'. It is a slow-growing shrub rather than a tree, wider than it is tall, up to about 10 ft (3 m) eventually and as much as 16 ft (5 m) wide.

The soft yellow foliage of *Acer shirasawanum* forma *aureum* remains effective throughout the summer

There are several coloured forms of *Thuja occidentalis*, but two of my favourites are 'Sunkist', a slow-growing dwarf conifer, up to 3 ft (1 m) or so, with a pyramidal habit, which retains its bright golden colouring reasonably well; and the well-known 'Rheingold', which is golden in the summer, turning to a coppery bronze in winter. This makes a slightly taller conifer than 'Sunkist', though slowly, so it is excellent as a pyramidal accent plant in a small garden.

There are other fine conifers but many, like the handsome *Chamaecyparis pisifera* 'Plumosa Aurea', acquire a distinctly greenish look as the season wears on. Some people enjoy the change because conifers can stay too much the same all year round; the trouble is that the yellow forms can look very washed out as the colour starts to fade.

DECIDUOUS TREES

Acer shirasawanum forma *aureum* is a good, yellow-leaved, small tree which retains its colour until leaf fall. It is slow-growing and therefore ideal for the smaller garden. This maple is best grown out of full sun, which would scorch the leaves, and does not thrive in a chalky soil.

Acer pseudoplatanus 'Worleei' makes a tree rather than a shrub, but is still less vigorous than the ordinary sycamore, growing to about 33 ft (10 m) in time. The golden yellow leaves turn green as the summer wears on.

Catalpa bignonioides 'Aurea' is the yellow-leaved form of the Indian bean tree. It will become a large spreading tree of 33 ft

Opposite: *Robinia pseudoacacia* 'Frisia', a graceful and distinctive small to medium-sized tree

(10 m) or more unless, as is sometimes recommended, it is pollarded by cutting it right back to a short stump in winter. If this is done, it will grow as a shrub and its huge, soft yellow, heart-shaped leaves can be associated with other garden plants. Where space is ample, I think it should be allowed to be a tree. The colour of the leaves remains until leaf fall, indeed, if anything, it gets better.

Fraxinus excelsior 'Jaspidea' is a form of the common ash which has golden yellow young shoots in spring and leaves turning yellow again in autumn. The bark is yellow as well, so it makes an interesting skeleton in winter. Ash trees are easy to grow, but should not be planted near buildings as they have far-searching roots and become very tall.

Gleditsia triacanthos 'Sunburst' is a revelation to those who see it for the first time. The pinnate leaves are attractive in themselves and they have the added charm of being the clearest brightest yellow. The yellowness does not remain and the flowers, unlike those of most members of the pea family, are insignificant, but I still think this small tree is worth growing, if you have room, for its spring splendour. It needs a sunny sheltered position in good soil.

Populus × *canadensis* 'Aurea' grows to 80 ft (25 m) or so, but can be stooled or pollarded, which is a good idea in small gardens. The heart-shaped glossy leaves are not so much yellow as yellow-green, but they turn properly yellow again before falling. Poplars are unfussy as to soil and thrive in damp conditions, but must be planted at least 65 ft (20 m) away from houses or drains.

Robinia pseudoacacia 'Frisia' is widely grown but I, for one, never tire of seeing it, particularly in the early autumn when the sulphur-yellow pinnate leaves turn more golden before falling. Like all acacia relatives (this goes for *Gleditsia* as well), it has brittle wood, so should be planted in a sheltered place. It grows to about 33 ft (10 m), making a broad-crowned tree. (See p.175.)

EVERGREEN SHRUBS

I can happily do without most of the yellow-leaved heaths and heathers because they look so awful when their pink or mauve flowers are out. But there are some, notably *Calluna vulgaris* 'Beoley Gold', which have white flowers. The combination is interesting and not unpleasant. When flowering in August and September, this calluna gets to about 1 ft (30 cm). It requires full sun and acid peaty soil.

Choisya ternata 'Sundance' is the yellow-foliage form of the Mexican orange blossom. It is a most effective shrub in a sunny, sheltered, well-drained spot. It grows to about 3 ft (1 m) high and wide and has fragrant flowers in May. The foliage colour is good, although older leaves do go green.

Hebe armstrongii is one of those easy-to-grow, useful, dwarf, evergreen shrubs for which there is always a place in the garden. It is, like all hebes, questionably hardy in exposed positions or on heavy soils, but in full sun it lasts well enough. The foliage is hardly recognizable as that of a hebe, being of the 'whipcord' type, with tiny, overlapping, scale-like leaves which are golden-green in colour. The small white flowers in summer do not measurably improve its appearance. It grows up to about 2 ft (60 cm) eventually, with the same spread, and associates well with other foliage plants.

DECIDUOUS SHRUBS

Berberis thunbergii 'Aurea' is a desirable deciduous shrub, provided you do not mind a plant which gives up all pretence of having coloured leaves half way through the summer. It is slow-growing, eventually reaching 3 ft (1 m) or so. The habit is dense and basically upright, the stems deeply grooved and the round leaves are crowded on the branches, which are armed with sharp thorns. This is not a plant to tangle with unnecessarily. It does best in partial shade and a sheltered place, where the morning sun will not scorch the frosted shoots in early spring. It is easy enough to grow in ordinary garden soil. (See p.178.)

Cornus mas 'Aurea' is not widely available, but is well worth seeking out. It is a form of the cornelian cherry and has clusters of small yellow flowers early in the year before the leaves open. When the oval leaves appear, they are golden yellow all summer. It is a bushy shrub which grows to about 8 ft (2.5 m); it needs a sunny place to flower well.

Philadelphus coronarius 'Aureus' is a winner in the right place but difficult to manage. In too much sun, the leaves brown and curl up; in too much shade, they are lime-green. Even if you get the balance right, I think it is unattractive when it flowers, for white and yellow do not always go well together. I believe it is best to trim it in spring to prevent flowering; it can look very striking as a clipped specimen in grass. The mock oranges are not particular about soil.

Sambucus racemosa 'Plumosa Aurea' is another plant which should be prevented from flowering, as the panicles of yellow-white flowers do not look particularly good with the foliage. The divided, deeply incised, pointed leaves start off coppery and become yellow and, in the early summer, the young ones which

The yellow leaves of *Berberis thunbergii* 'Aurea' turn pale green by late summer

are still growing contrast with those which are mature. The elder can be hacked about without hurt so, if you do not like the panicles of flowers in April and May, cut it back hard in the winter.

Spiraea japonica 'Goldflame' is a vogue plant which pleases me early in the season, but less so as the golden yellow colour becomes more dispersed and the rose-red flowers are borne in late summer. However, it will grow in some shade and is not more than 3 ft (1 m) in height even when established. It is useful, hardy and uncomplaining.

PERENNIALS

Filipendula ulmaria 'Aurea' is the yellow-leaved meadowsweet and a good choice for a shady moist spot. It is usually recommended that one remove the creamy white flowers to encourage new golden leaves to grow in the autumn and to prevent the older leaves from turning green, but the flowers are so sweetly

Filipendula ulmaria 'Aurea', a delightful form of the native meadowsweet or queen of the meadows

scented that it rather goes against the grain to do so. This plant grows to about 1½ ft (45 cm); the leaves are pinnate and deeply veined and held on horizontal stems.

Humulus lupulus 'Aureus', the yellow-leaved version of the hop, is a vigorous herbaceous climber and looks particularly good on the wall of a limestone or pale-bricked house. The leaves are coarsely toothed, furrowed, in three lobes and golden yellow. It can also be allowed to scramble through a loose shrub or up a tree or over a hedge. It is not as often enough grown as it deserves. It does best in a good moisture-retentive soil.

Milium effusum aureum is known as Bowles' golden grass, after E. A. Bowles, the great amateur botanist and plantsman, who popularized it. It is always a pleasure to come across this plant lighting up a shady corner in an enthusiast's garden. It makes a small clump of upright leaves, only about 1 ft (30 cm) high; even the "flower" stems, which are also yellow, reach only about 1¼ ft (40 cm) and are very delicate. It seeds about a little, quite inoffensively. (See p.180.)

Bowles' golden grass is a useful golden-leaved plant for a shady situation

The golden marjoram, *Origanum vulgare* 'Aureum', is not a thrilling plant but it is a cheerful body for a quite sunny place and has the bonus of being a culinary herb. It gets no higher than 1 ft (30 cm) and is very useful as groundcover or as edging for a border.

Valeriana phu 'Aurea' loses its bright golden colour in a few weeks, yet while at its best it is irresistible and afterwards it blends in pleasantly enough. Unlike the wall valerian, which can be such a nuisance, this is a well-behaved plant. It has 3 ft (1 m) stems of small white flowers in June, which may need staking, but it is for the yellow elliptical base leaves and deeply cut stem leaves that we grow it. This is a plant to consider if you have room for something which does not pay its way all year.

Variegated Foliage

Variegation, that is, the presence of two or more colours in a leaf, is a common occurrence in plants. There are many different combinations – cream and green; yellow and green; pink, green and white; even, in the case of *Hydrangea macrophylla* 'Quadricolor', yellow, cream, grey and green. The leaf of *Ajuga reptans* 'Multicolor' is a strange concoction of red, pink, cream-yellow and bronze. In some plants, the colour other than green is on the margin, for instance, *Elaeagnus × ebbingei* 'Gilt Edge'; in others it is in the middle, as in *Elaeagnus pungens* 'Maculata'. Some leaves are splashed, some speckled, some mottled. The variations of variegation all make for great fun for the gardener, although variegated plants are not always easy to place.

Variegations arise for a number of reasons, but most often as a result of a genetic mutation which has occurred in a green-leaved plant. That being so, reversion back to plain green leaves is a constant danger and, when seen, must be removed, otherwise the superior vigour of the green plant will swamp the variegated parts. Variegated plants are, generally speaking, not as strong-growing nor as sturdy as green plants, so they need more careful attention and placing. From the aesthetic angle, too, one must be careful not to over-use variegated plants, for a little goes a long way.

DECIDUOUS TREES

Acer platanoides 'Drummondii' is a striking variegated tree, much planted by local authorities in public parks. Unfortunately, the leaves revert all too easily and the aforementioned councils rarely get round to cutting off the offending branches. It has distinctive white margins to the pointed leaves and is less vigorous than the ordinary Norway maple, rarely attaining even 50 ft (15 m) and 33 ft (10 m) across. It is a good choice for a specimen tree.

Populus candicans 'Aurora' is also a good specimen tree and, being a poplar, it can be stooled or pollarded every year in March if you wish to make the most of the heart-shaped leaves. It is the youngest of these which are the most colourful; they are green, splashed and marbled with creamy white and pink. (See p.183.)

181

EVERGREEN SHRUBS

The spotted laurels are on my list of least desirable shrubs, for the combination of yellow speckling on dark green leaves, with anaemic young growths, is awful. However, I concede that they will grow even in polluted atmospheres and in dry shade, where nothing much else will prosper, and there is one, Aucuba japonica 'Picturata', which is very much better than the rest. The leaves are properly splashed instead of just being spattered. The two sexes are on different bushes, but I should not bother to grow more than one, as the red berries add a discordant note.

There are no more garden-worthy foliage shrubs than the evergreen elaeagnus, particularly the variegated forms; they are always striking, seeming brightest in the winter, and they are unfussy about soil or position. Elaeagnus pungens 'Maculata' has glossy green leaves with great splashes of butter-yellow in the middle, whereas Elaeagnus × ebbingei 'Gilt Edge' has the yellow along the margins. Both get to be quite large shrubs in time if you are not tempted to remove all the branches for flower arranging. (I do not know what flower arrangers did before these shrubs became widely available.)

There are some good forms of Euonymus fortunei var. radicans, some of which trail and some of which make humpy little shrubs. 'Emerald 'n' Gold' and 'Emerald Gaiety' are two of the latter. I grow them together and, although they have been slow to get going and have never gone beyond 1½ ft (45 cm), they do complement each other quite well. The first is green with an irregular, greeny yellow margin, the second green with a white irregular margin. The leaves take on a pinkish tinge in cold weather. They will grow in sun or part shade and in any reasonable soil.

Griselinia littoralis 'Variegata' is only reliably hardy on the coast, where frosts are uncommon, while its glossy leaves can withstand the salt spray. The variegation consists of great splashes of creamy white on the green leaves. If winters are mild, this shrub will grow to about 6 ft (2 m) and 4 ft (1.2 m) across. It is striking enough for any gardener to wish to take a chance with it in a warm spot.

There are so many variegated ivies it is hard to decide which of them merit inclusion. Hedera colchica 'Dentata Variegata' is certainly one of my favourites. The leaves are basically dark green, with light green and creamy yellow markings. They are very large, up to 8 in. (20 cm) long and 7 in. (18 cm) wide. This vigorous climber looks well growing over a tree stump or up a wall, even one facing north. Hedera algeriensis 'Gloire de Marengo' ('Variegata') is not dissimilar, except that the marginal variegation is creamy white. It is less hardy. These two ivies look good together.

Above (left): The variegation of *Populus candicans* 'Aurora' develops best on long shoots; (right) *Aucuba japonica* 'Picturata' has conspicuous yellow marking on the leaves
Below (left): *Ilex × altaclerensis* 'Golden King', an outstanding variegated holly; (right) *Lonicera japonica* 'Aureoreticulata' is ideal as a climber or as groundcover

So do the much smaller-leaved *Hedera helix* ssp. *helix* 'Orodi Bogliasco' ('Goldheart') which has a big splash of yellow in the centre of the triangular leaves, and 'Buttercup', which is all yellow and, therefore, not very vigorous. These ivies are self-clinging once established, which is a boon for the busy gardener or for anyone whose house walls will not take nails easily.

Ilex × altaclerensis 'Golden King' is a fine holly which can attain 23 ft (7 m) with a spread of 16 ft (5 m) but, like all variegated hollies, can be painfully slow to grow. The leaves are scarcely spiny, which is nice, and have golden yellow margins. It is a female, I have to say, which means large red berries in autumn. These frankly do not improve the look of it, but they are usually quite quickly eaten by the birds. (See p.183) This holly looks effective grouped with white-variegated ones like *Ilex aquifolium* 'Silver Milkmaid' or 'Silver Queen'. The former has the white splash in the centre, whereas the latter has white margins. Both of these are male and do not produce berries.

Ligustrum ovalifolium 'Aureum', the golden privet, is closely related to the much despised common privet and itself comes in for some criticism. However, it grows less quickly, so does not have quite the same demand for trimming, and the colour is very bright and cheering. As a free-standing bush, it will get up to 6 ft (2 m) or so and, if allowed to flower, it has white panicles in July. The scent is too heavy for my taste. The leaf which is, naturally enough, oval, is yellow except for the very middle where it is green. It is semi-evergreen.

Lonicera japonica 'Aureo-reticulata' has, as its name suggests, leaves netted with gold on all the veins; this characteristic gives it a most unusual look for a honeysuckle. It is a vigorous climber but needs a sunny position and, even so, may lose its leaves in harsh winters. It does flower in summer but not very significantly or generously. The flowers are yellow and scented. (See p.183.)

Pieris japonica 'Variegata' is a startling plant. It has narrower oval leaves than its wholly green counterpart and the margins are creamy yellow. The young leaves are flushed with pink. It makes a dense shrub and is a slow grower which will reach 10 ft (3 m) eventually. Unfortunately, it is a resolute lime-hater.

One of the loveliest variegated shrubs is *Rhamnus alaternus* 'Argenteovariegata'. This reasonably fast-growing evergreen has small, oval, grey-green leaves with irregular, creamy white margins. It gives of its best in full sun.

Salvia officinalis 'Icterina' and 'Tricolor' are both delightful. 'Icterina' is the golden sage and its new foliage is yellow, gold and grey-green. 'Tricolor' is white, pink and purple. These do not go well together, although it would be convenient if they did because

Left: *Salvia officinalis* 'Tricolor', with *Teucrium pyrenaicum* in the corner
Right: *Thymus* × *citriodorus* 'Silver Queen', a variegated form of the lemon thyme

---

they both grow to 2 ft (60 cm) and need full sun, a well-drained soil and a trim over in spring.

There are not very many variegated rock plants but *Thymus* × *citriodorus* 'Silver Queen' is a good one. The grey-green and silver leaves go well with the pale lilac flowers. This ground-hugging sub-shrub needs a sunny well-drained place to thrive and a trim over after flowering. If any branches revert to green, they should be cut out.

The creeping *Vinca major* 'Variegata' is not so rampageous as *Vinca minor*, but it nevertheless must be watched. It makes rotten groundcover because it has long trailing stems which root at the ends, but it is an agreeable plant to allow to wander about in an unappealing spot in dry semi-shade. The glossy oval leaves are grey-green with creamy yellow variegations. There are blue-mauve, star-shaped, periwinkle flowers in April and May and sometimes also in late summer.

DECIDUOUS SHRUBS

Actinidia kolomikta is a glorious and unusual climber. Related to the Chinese gooseberry, it has heart-shaped leaves, up to 6 in. (15 cm) long, which begin purplish green but, as the season wears on, develop variegations – white on the pointed end of the leaves and pink nearer the centre. Sometimes the whole leaf colours, particularly if the climber is in a warm sunny spot. It is not always an easy plant to keep alive, especially in the north. It is never very vigorous and needs good support for the twining stems. (See p. 187.)

185

Berberis thunbergii 'Rose Glow' is a very popular shrub and rightly so, although it can be difficult to place it happily. This is particularly true in spring when the leaves are splashed with different shades of pink as well as purple. Later in the season, the leaves are simply purple. 'Harlequin' is quite similar, but has white speckles. These are slower-growing than the ordinary *B. thunbergii* and they will reach 4 ft (1.2 m) in a few years.

Cornus alba 'Spaethii' and 'Elegantissima' are variegated forms of the red-stemmed dogwood. The first has golden-variegated leaves, the second white mottlings and margins. They both grow up to about 8 ft (2.5 m) and, though it is tempting to try them together, they do not look especially good side by side. Being dogwoods, they like a moisture-retentive soil in sun or partial shade. They should be hard pruned in spring for maximum decorative effect.

Fuchsia magellanica 'Versicolor' lives up to its name and is graceful but not very vigorous. The leaves are a satisfactory mixture of colours – grey-green, pink and creamy white, particularly on the young shoots. The form *gracilis* 'Variegata' has creamy yellow margins, but is less strong in constitution even than 'Versicolor'. Both have slender red and purple flowers and grow best in a sheltered sunny place. These shrubs are usually cut down by frost in winter but, once established, are unlikely to be killed by it. They are choice enough to deserve protection anyway.

Hypericum × moserianum 'Tricolor' has very interesting variegation, namely, grey-green leaves with reddish pink and white markings. This is not especially enhanced by the long-lasting yellow flowers. It is a small, open, even a little scruffy, shrub, which sends up arching stems to about 2 ft (60 cm) and flowers from July until October. It may die back in winter and new growth will not emerge until May.

Parthenocissus henryana is a self-clinging relation of the Virginia creeper, with dark green, five-lobed leaves which have silvery pink veins. It is a very vigorous climber, but requires some shelter, relishing a west or north west wall. The variegation becomes more pronounced as autumn approaches and the leaves turn bright red before falling. No one notices the flowers at midsummer.

Symphoricarpos orbiculatus 'Foliis Variegatus' is a great improvement on the very dull, green snowberry. It is a dense shrub with leaves which are round and irregularly margined with yellow. Do not plant it in too shady a place or the variegation will be less obvious and may disappear. The flowers are pale pink and the berries purplish red.

Above (left): *Actinidia kolomikta* should be grown on a sunny wall for the most pronounced variegation; (right) the silvery markings of *Parthenocissus henryana* are more strongly defined in partial shade
Below: *Berberis thunbergii* 'Rose Glow', a charming small shrub introduced in 1965

Left: A remarkable mixture of colours in the foliage of *Ajuga reptans* 'Multicolor'
Right: *Pleioblastus auricomus* is a beautiful sight in full leaf in late summer

PERENNIALS

Ajuga reptans 'Multicolor' has received a mention in the introduction to this chapter for the amount of colours to be discerned on the leaf. The flowers are the typical blue-mauve bugle flowers in April and May. There is another form called 'Variegata' which has creamy white margins to the grey-green leaves. Both make good groundcover in rich soil and semi-shade.

Carex morrowii 'Evergold' is a sedge with evergreen arching leaves up to 8 in. (20 cm) long; these are golden yellow with thin green margins. It always looks neat whatever the time of year and very much appreciates a moist position.

Fragaria vesca 'Variegata' is the variegated wild strawberry. It has a fresh bright look about it because of the uneven splashes of creamy white on a dark green background. It likes to be in part-shade and will meander about agreeably without becoming a menace.

Glyceria maxima 'Variegata' thrives in heavy moist soil, for it is really a waterside grass, and it can become unmanageable if the conditions suit. However, it will survive quite well in dryish soil. The leaves are pinkish in spring, then striped green, yellow and white when mature, on stems up to 4 ft (1.2 m).

There are so many good variegated hostas that a favourite is hard to choose, but I do think *Hosta sieboldiana* 'Frances Williams' is exceptional. The leaves are dark blue-green and corrugated, with thick yellow margins. It really is a good colour combination. There are other worthy ones, like *Hosta ventricosa*

188

Left: *Hosta sieboldiana* 'Frances Williams', originally known as 'Gold Edge'
Right: *Iris pallida* 'Variegata' has very effective white-striped leaves

'Variegata', which has yellow- or cream-margined foliage with good blue flowers in late summer; and the similar *Hosta crispula* with white-edged leaves.

Iris pallida 'Variegata' is just one of several good white- or yellow-striped irises. It has pretty blue-mauve flowers in June. It needs a reasonably sunny well-drained place to thrive. *Iris pseudacorus* 'Variegata', on the other hand, which has yellow-striped leaves, flourishes in bogs or shallow water. It produces yellow flowers in June, after which the variegation on the leaves fades.

Miscanthus sinensis 'Variegatus' and 'Zebrinus' are two forms of a very useful, tall, ornamental grass. The first grows to about 5 ft (1.5 m), the second a little more, but neither is invasive. 'Zebrinus', the zebra grass, has yellow bands on the green leaves after midsummer, whereas 'Variegatus' has white stripes. They have feathery flower heads in October. They do best in moist soil, in sun or part-shade.

Molinia caerulea var. *caerulea* 'Variegata' is a grass with neat foliage, up to 1½ ft (45 cm) high, and feathery flower stems, up to 3 ft (1 m), in autumn. The leaves are thin, first erect and then arching, and green striped with cream. This is another plant for a moist soil in sun or semi-shade.

Persicaria virginiana 'Painter's Palette' has branching stems of oval leaves, splashed with pink, grey and cream. There is a distinctive deep red 'V' in the middle of each leaf. The flowers are insignificant. It likes a rich soil in semi-shade.

Above: The striking *Symphytum* × *uplandicum* 'Variegatum' appreciates some shade
Below: *Silybum marianum* will grow in any ordinary soil

Phormium cookianum ssp. *hookeri* 'Cream Delight' is one of the best of these not very hardy New Zealand flaxes. Generally speaking, phormiums are not plants for cold places but, if you have a sheltered warm position in a moisture-retentive soil, this one grows to about 3 ft (1 m) and has a cream band in the centre of the ascending leaves, which bend over towards the top. It is smaller than *Phormium tenax* and, to my mind, less bizarre as an accent plant.

Pleioblastus auricomus is a bamboo which grows to about 4 ft (1.2 m). The leaves are green with yellow stripes; the variegation is brightest in full sun. This is one of the better-behaved bamboos because it is clump-forming and therefore not invasive.

Symphytum × *uplandicum* 'Variegatum' is very robust and well-variegated all summer. This plant looks best when the mauve and pink flowers are not out. It makes a basal rosette up to 3 ft (1 m) of large, sage-green, grey- and cream-margined, oval, hairy leaves.

Sedum telephium 'Variegatum' is a curious rather than strictly pretty version of the ice plant. The leaves are blue-green with creamy yellow variegations; the flowers in late summer are pink. All-green shoots are apt to appear and have to be cut out. It grows to about 1¼ ft (40 cm) tall and looks best in a group.

BIENNIALS

Silybum marianum is a very exciting plant, even if it is meat and drink to aphids. It is known as Our Lady's milk thistle and, if you let it, has tall heads of mauve thistle flowers. The oval lobed leaves in a basal rosette are a dark shiny green, heavily marbled with white veins. This is a biennial but, unfortunately, it is not available from all seedsmen. However, it is worth seeking out.

191

Ground Cover Plants

Compiled by the Wisley Gardens Staff of The Royal Horticultural Society

This ground cover scheme in spring includes hardy geraniums, hellebores, *Skimmia japonica* and the newly emerged foliage of peonies

Introduction

Ground cover is a term that has been used often in the horticultural literature of the last thirty years. It is a technique of growing plants close together so that they make a continuous canopy of leaves over the soil. This canopy must be thick enough to prevent any other plants (i.e. weeds) from becoming established below it. The weeds will not thrive chiefly because of lack of light, but also because of root competition for water and nutrients. This situation is natural in the wild, where plants most suited to a particular environment will survive, flourish and smother the weaker plants. The difference in the garden is that the gardener, not the environment, chooses what is to grow and survive.

A garden is an artificial environment. Almost all our garden plants have been either introduced from other climates or bred for characters that would not necessarily allow them to survive in the wild in this country. All cultivation of garden plants is directed at creating and maintaining an artificial population. But in doing this it is sensible to adopt natural methods, as in the ground cover approach.

The theory of ground cover, therefore, is to use ornamental plants to cover areas of soil in the garden so thickly that no weeds can compete. In the modern interpretation the plants used must be those that can thrive with only minimum maintenance. Neither grass nor carpet bedding qualify, because although they fulfil the first requirement they need a lot of labour – grass must be regularly mowed to keep it looking controlled, and carpet bedding needs even more work in the annual production of new plants. The types of plant which do qualify are perennial and hardy for the area where they are to grow.

Although the technique is not really a new one, it is particularly applicable to modern gardens with little available labour, and where there are fairly large areas which can sensibly and attractively be devoted to ground cover plants. In general, appropriate plants are relatively low and spreading; those with upright, open-branched growth are unsuitable as they do not exclude light from the soil surface and allow weeds to flourish. There is no clear

Opposite: The lesser periwinkle, *Vinca minor*, and its forms are some of the most efficient ground covers

Stachys olympica 'Silver Carpet' lives up to its name in a sunny position

dividing line between plants that are good as ground cover and those that are not. In between come many plants whose effectiveness as ground cover depends on the gardener and on the environment. Choosing suitable plants for the conditions and encouraging them to grow well are important factors for success with ground cover.

Some enthusiasts give the impression that almost all members of the plant kingdom can be used as ground cover. In practice, only a proportion are satisfactory. When starting with ground cover in the garden, it is better to choose easily controlled and easily cultivated plants and a selection is given on pp.212–248. All have their disadvantages as well as advantages. Either they are easy to establish and will continue growing vigorously so that later they need to be restrained, or they need a good deal of attention to get them to flourish. Some start off well and are excellent for a year or two but then gradually deteriorate. Be prepared for some degree of compromise, according to the situation and conditions of the individual garden.

Why Use Ground Cover?

The main reason for using ground cover is to reduce the time spent on keeping the ground clear of weeds between the desirable plants. The effect of a complete carpet of plants also gives an attractive natural appearance.

Most people will still want some area of lawn in the garden, for sitting out, and no other ground cover has such tolerance to human traffic. But there are many places where ground cover can be recommended instead of grass. In shade, for instance, grass will rarely grow well, whereas numerous ground cover plants will thrive. Shade beneath trees is particularly difficult, partly because of competing roots and partly because the light conditions beneath a tree will change as the tree grows, and so after a few years the plants chosen initially for light shade may need to be replaced by others that will tolerate denser shade. (See also the section on plants for shade, pp. 77–133.)

The purple-leaved *Viola labradorica* and the foam flower, *Tiarella cordifolia*, thrive in shade

Grass banks are another problem garden feature, being both awkward and often dangerous to mow. An alternative is to plant permanent ground cover, which may also help to stabilize the bank and prevent soil erosion.

Shrub (including rose) borders too can be planted with lower ground cover plants to give a pleasing community of varying heights. There is one snag that may arise and that is to keep the shrubs sufficiently well fed. With such a dense community of competing plants, regular feeding is essential. Foliar nutrition may also be useful (see p.210).

Ground cover plants can be used almost anywhere in the garden – to edge beds and borders, in a rock garden and over large areas which might otherwise be time-consuming to maintain. Often we achieve 'ground cover' without realising it, but to be effective it usually requires careful planning, together with the right selection of plants for the aspect and soil.

The rose of Sharon, *Hypericum calycinum*, has become naturalised in parts of Britain

What Can Be Used?

Plants suitable for ground cover are by definition perennials, that is, shrubs or herbaceous plants. Annuals and biennials are too short-lived to compete with weeds, although there may sometimes be a place for a spreading low-growing annual such as *Limnanthes douglasii* as a 'filler' in the first year between the permanent perennials.

Almost any plant which has a spreading habit of growth is in its way acting as ground cover. Although many plants are recommended, it is as well to realise that a considerable number – hellebores, pulsatillas, *Claytonia sibirica* and various rock plants like *Acantholimon* among them – which are sometimes suggested, do not really fulfil the function of ground cover as defined here, either because the foliage canopy they make is not dense enough to suppress the weeds effectively, or because it is very slow to cover the ground.

The main requirements of a good ground cover plant are:

(a) Hardiness, in an average winter, in the area concerned. As an example, *Hypericum calycinum* is usually hardy throughout Britain. *Osteospermum* (*Dimorphotheca*) 'Nairobi Purple', although an excellent ground cover, is less likely to survive the winter at the RHS Garden, Wisley, than in Cornwall where winters are usually less severe.

(b) Tolerance of other adverse conditions, particularly periods of drought or extended wet weather.

(c) Sufficient vigour to cover the available ground in the first or second season after planting.

(d) The ability to form a dense, relatively low-growing cover and to remain in good condition for a number of years (at least 5 to 10) without requiring very much attention. Evergreens may be more effective in fulfilling this requirement, as deciduous plants, such as hostas, allow annual weeds (chickweed, cleavers, and grass) to grow after the foliage has died down and particularly in early spring before their leaves have developed fully to cover the ground again.

(e) A degree of beauty and interest as a garden plant during the year. Attractive flowers and/or fruits at some season, or foliage which is interesting in shape, pattern, texture or colour are very desirable. Good foliage, particularly of evergreens, which will be seen by the gardener throughout the

The hummock-forming *Ceanothus thyrsiflorus* var. *repens* is a hardy and attractive evergreen shrub

year, is most important.

(f) Low maintenance. An annual feeding or top-dressing and a clip-over or removal of dying foliage are all that should be needed. The plant should also be more or less free of the usual pests and diseases – spraying is work and costs money. Some evergreen ground covers (and also deciduous plants like hostas) in damp conditions are havens for slugs and snails, which will require control.

There is a wide range of plants, both woody and herbaceous, which fulfil these requirements. However, the particular garden conditions in which the plants are to be grown should also be considered and the gardener must make the best of the situation and the plants available.

Garden Conditions

Every garden is different, in soil, in climate, and in man-made features such as walls and their effect on the environment. These conditions can be altered to some extent, but a less laborious way of gardening is to choose plants that will grow well in the existing conditions, or with some relatively minor amendments to them.

First, these conditions must be analysed. In a small garden there will be quite a variation in the microclimate, even in the course of one day. One part has morning sun, one has evening sun, another has sun all day, or no sun at all. Combine these variations with those of rainfall, frost, wind during the year, and soil, and it is clear that plants must be able to adapt to a range of conditions.

Rainfall cannot be controlled but can be supplemented if necessary by watering. The amount of sunshine in a particular position can be exploited by using plants that like the sun or those that grow best in the shade. Similarly, wind-tolerant plants can be chosen for very exposed gardens. Frost should only be a problem in exceptional years if hardy plants are grown.

Soils can be improved, although it takes time. The ideal soil for most plants is a neutral loam, neither too light in texture (sand) nor too heavy (clay). There are few ideal soils, but much can be done to improve soil texture, primarily by adding humus (see p.206). Any type of humus can be used; garden compost, farmyard manure, leafmould, pulverised bark, mushroom compost (which is often alkaline), and peat are among suitable types most often available.

Less can be done to alter soil alkalinity or acidity, and it is a long-term process, so it is simpler to choose plants that are suited to the existing soil conditions – ericas, for example, on acid soils.

'Annemarie', one of the numerous cultivars of *Calluna vulgaris*

Above: The distinctive foliage of *Hosta undulata* var. *univittata* with a broad cream stripe in the centre
Below: 'Coral Beauty', a recently introduced form of the carpeting *Cotoneaster dammeri*

—— Types of Ground Cover Plants ——

There are two main groups of herbaceous ground covers – clump-formers; and carpeters or colonisers. The first are relatively slow and steady growers, the second are fast growing but may in some instances produce a thinner canopy. Under 'herbaceous' are included bergenias and some epimediums, which keep their leaves over the winter, and therefore are not strictly herbaceous.

Shrubs too can be grouped in broadly the same way – those that produce a dense network of branches to form hummocks over several years; and those which spread more rapidly by rooting into the soil as they travel, or by producing suckers from underground roots.

For the purposes of this book, ground cover plants have been divided into six groups according to the type of cover they make. These divisions are arbitrary, and some overlap is inevitable.

A. Quick growing evergreens with dense twiggy growth, either carpeters or colonisers. These are the most efficient ground covers, and will make an almost complete canopy in the first year after planting at the distances recommended. Examples are certain cultivars of ivy, *Hedera helix*, and forms of the lesser periwinkle, *Vinca minor*.

B. Evergreens of dense growth which will take two seasons to cover the ground completely at the distances recommended. Alternatively, but more expensively, they can be planted closer together to obtain a good canopy in the first year. They may need extra encouragement, such as pruning, to stimulate more branching near the soil surface. *Erica herbacea* (*E.carnea*), dwarf junipers and *Alyssum* (*Aurinia*) *saxatilis* are examples of these hummock-forming or slow carpeting or colonising plants.

C. Deciduous clump-forming plants, which make thick cover with their leaves during the growing season, but die down during winter. Although there is no cover at that time their dense network of roots competes to some extent with annual weeds that may try to grow in the winter; but they are not completely effective ground covers and early spring weeding to remove weeds such as chickweed and annual meadow grass is often necessary. These are the slow but steady herbaceous type; examples are *Hemerocallis* (daylilies), hostas, *Alchemilla mollis* and geraniums such as *G. wallichianum* which, although wide spreading, does not (or very rarely) root at the nodes.

203

D. Carpeters or colonisers, deciduous or evergreen, which either make a network of stems over the ground, rooting into the soil as they travel, or send out stolons or sucker growths, often from their roots. These often cover the soil area rapidly, but not all make such a dense cover as groups A to C, even in summer. Eventually they form thick mats of growth but during the first season before cover is complete they are likely to need regular weeding. Examples are *Duchesnea* (*Fragaria*) *indica*, *Glechoma hederacea* 'Variegata' and acaenas.

E. Trailers which do not generally branch and root so much but have an 'umbrella-spoke' habit; they may be deciduous or evergreen. Because of their long growths these plants take longer than the earlier groups to make a thick cover and the gardener needs to have patience. Examples are *Rosa* 'Max Graf' and *Clematis*. They have the considerable drawback of requiring at least two years of weed control and this is not always easy to carry out. In some situations, particularly on banks, they have their uses, but it is essential to deal with the weeds initially if they are to be successful.

F. A last group may be mentioned, but with reservations. It consists of plants which are often so vigorous that unless regularly restrained they may swamp their neighbours. Such plants can sometimes be more trouble than they are worth, because of the amount of attention they need. Among them we include the various climbers sometimes suggested (e.g. the honeysuckles, *Lonicera japonica halliana* and *L. henryi*) which make a good canopy, but need considerable and regular control, unless they are planted in areas where they have room to spread without strangling their neighbours.

The aim of this book is to guide gardeners to plants that will be effective without constantly needing long-term attention and the list on pp.212–248 contains a selection of the most satisfactory and reliable plants for the purpose.

Preparing and Planting

To grow any plant successfully a favourable environment needs to be created and maintained. Almost all garden plants are incomers, expected to grow in an unaccustomed climate and to compete with the natives, which are well adapted to the environment. The chosen plants need all the help they can get from the gardener to become established and to flourish.

Having decided where the plants are to grow, the next requirements are to provide a soil bed in good condition for plant growth, and to remove all competitors, i.e. weeds. It is particularly important to eliminate perennial weeds before planting because afterwards it is almost impossible to get out the deep-rooting and persistent weeds without disturbing the other plants.

CONTROL OF ANNUAL WEEDS

Annual weeds are a relatively straightforward problem as they are mostly shallow-rooting and can be easily removed when forking over the soil before planting.

Once ground cover plants are well established they should provide a cover sufficiently dense to inhibit or prevent germination of weed seeds, but weed control may be necessary in the first season or two after planting, using mulches or by careful hoeing.

CONTROL OF PERENNIAL WEEDS

It cannot be overemphasised that it is essential to remove all perennial weeds before planting any areas of ground cover. Perennial weeds such as ground elder, couch grass and bindweed will compete with ground cover and are almost impossible to control once ground cover has been planted. Where the ground is infested with such persistent weeds, there should be no plans for planting until they have been completely removed.

Both mechanical and chemical methods can be used to remove perennial weeds. Allow a reasonable interval between treatment and planting so that if the weeds have not been completely eliminated there is an opportunity to see and treat any regrowth. By mechanical methods is meant weed removal by hand, by hoe, spade or machine. The last is only feasible before planting; the second and third are not recommended after planting, and the first can be done at any time.

Chemical herbicides must always be used very carefully, and at the correct time of year. Glyphosate is particularly useful against difficult perennial weeds, applied between July and September. Care must be taken that it does not come in contact with cultivated plants. (For further information see the Wisley Handbook, *Weed Control in the Garden*.)

PREPARATION OF THE SOIL

Many people believe that ground cover plants will grow without any particular care in soil preparation. This is a fallacy and may account for the poor results obtained with ground cover in some cases. Proper preparation of the soil is just as important for ground cover plants, if they are to grow well and remain in good condition for some years, as it is for roses.

A soil which is naturally fertile and of good structure is exceptional and most soils will benefit considerably from the incorporation of humus of some type in the top soil layer. The humus is dug in to a spade's depth, preferably in autumn, and the surface is left in a rough condition to weather over the winter.

Humus will improve most soil types, especially if applied regularly, increasing the water-holding capacity of light soils, improving the drainage of heavier soils and providing some of the main nutrients for the plants. But nutrients are present in humus in only relatively small amounts (and hardly at all in most peats) and become available only slowly. An extra supply of nutrients will help plants to become established more quickly, and a general balanced fertilizer, such as Growmore, can be applied before planting, at a rate of 1 to 2 oz per square yard (33 to 66 g per m²).

PLANTING

Now that plants are available in containers at all times of year, they can be planted at any season, but they must be cared for after planting, particularly in hot and dry weather, to make sure that they do not suffer from lack of water. The best time for planting is late autumn, or better still, early spring, when the soil is starting to warm up and usually contains plenty of moisture, which will soon encourage the roots to grow.

The method is the same for all plants. Dig a hole wide enough to take the roots without cramping them and deep enough to take the roots or the soil ball, so that the newly planted plant is at the same level in the border as it was in the nursery or container. With container plants it is easy to see that they are neither too deep nor too

Ground cover plants may look sparse at first, as with *Helianthemum nummularium* 'Amy Baring' (above), but the aim should be to achieve a dense effect such as that of *Hebe rakaiensis* (below)

high; the soil level in the container is the guide. With bare-root shrubs there will be a mark on the stem showing the level of the soil in the nursery before lifting, and the soil after planting in the new position should come to the same level. With bare-root herbaceous plants, the collar of the plant, where roots and shoots join, should be at soil level. When planting bare-root plants do not allow the roots to dry out while they are waiting to be put in – sun and spring winds can sometimes dry out fibrous roots very quickly, so cover the roots with some sheeting or sacking.

When the plant is in the right position, replace the soil and firm it in well all round, finally forking over the surface to make it look tidy.

Spacing at the planting stage depends on the following factors:

1. Type of ground cover (see p.203) i.e. how quickly the plants will cover a given area.
2. Ultimate spread of the plants. This is influenced to some extent by the environmental conditions, e.g. the fertility of the soil.
3. Size of the plants at planting. (See also the list, pp.212–248, for recommended planting distances.)

All these factors need to be correlated to determine the spacing, for the sooner the neighbouring plants meet, the better for weed control. Smaller, younger plants tend to grow more rapidly than larger, older plants because of their greater vigour. But the size of the plants and their cost do also have a bearing on the spacing and eventual coverage. Eight small plants spaced at 18 inches (45 cm) apart may cover the same area more efficiently in the first season than six large plants, planted 3 ft (0.9 m) apart. However, when planting a larger area it may be too expensive to plant for the optimum effect as soon as possible, and so the plants are put in at wider spacing, with the commitment to continue weeding for two seasons instead of one.

Many nursery catalogues give an indication of the spread of the plants, and if buying from a reliable garden centre there should be someone who can guide the buyer on this. It is a good idea to see the plants growing in other people's gardens; or to visit a ground cover demonstration plot such as those at the RHS Garden at Wisley in Surrey, at Probus, near Bodmin, Cornwall, and at the Royal Botanic Garden in Edinburgh.

Maintenance

WEED CONTROL

Once the plants are in, the weed control programme needs to be started and continued regularly, either by hoeing, by herbicides (see p.206), by interplanting (e.g. with annuals) or by mulching. In the first year after planting it is vital to give consistent weed control so that any competition for nutrients and water by other plants is kept to a minimum.

For annual weeds, hoeing or removal by hand as soon as they are seen is the most effective method. If this is done regularly as the seedlings germinate then there should be no problem. Any persistent perennial weeds, such as dandelions and nettles, which may have escaped the initial clearance can be treated with a weedkiller like glyphosate.

MULCHING

A layer 2 to 3 in. (5–7.5 cm) thick of mulching material placed between the freshly planted ground cover is an excellent method of suppressing weed growth and it is beneficial in encouraging the rapid development of the plants. It is important to ensure that the mulch is not contaminated with weed seeds (often a problem with home-made compost) and to remember that many types of mulch are excellent seed beds for wind-blown seeds. But it may be a consolation that the seedlings that do germinate in a good mulch often grow so lushly that they are easy to pluck out. Peat and pulverised bark and any of the materials mentioned on p.201 may be used for mulching. Black polythene is also an effective mulching material.

It is important that the mulch goes between the plants and not on top of the growing shoots of the herbaceous plants which may be smothered themselves. Regular mulching in spring between the clump-formers until they meet will help weed control and also improve the humus content of the soil. Once they have spread into each other it is difficult to get the mulch beneath the plants and on to the soil. A thick layer of mulching material should not be put on top of carpeters or colonisers because it would smother them, but a thinner layer sprinkled between the stems each year in spring will help to keep some humus supplied to the soil.

Woodland plants such as *Pulmonaria angustifolia* benefit particularly
from a mulch

FERTILIZING

Fertilizers are not often applied to ground cover in gardens but
they should be and will improve growth, and keep it vigorous.
Early spring is the time to apply most fertilizers, either a general
artificial fertilizer such as Growmore or an organic fertilizer such
as bone meal. Slow-release fertilizers can also be very useful.
They are more expensive than other fertilizers, but are formulated
to release nutrients into the soil over a much longer period. Apply
the fertilizer carefully to the soil around the plants in spring,
taking care to avoid the foliage as some artificial fertilizers may
scorch the leaves.

Foliar feeding is sometimes recommended for plants. This is
the application of a diluted liquid feed by spraying on to the leaves
which quickly take in the nutrients. Foliar feeding will produce a
rapid response from the plant, if applied at the right time, and
quickly stimulates plant growth. The most effective times to apply
foliar feeds are in late spring and early summer, when extension
growth is normally being produced.

The main value of foliar feeding is to reinvigorate and feed
plants that are backward in growth, such as those with a poor root

The questing roots of *Hemerocallis fulva* will colonise large areas, but other daylilies form more manageable clumps

system (perhaps due to drought) or those that are not yet established. It can also be useful as a quick feed for shrubs in a border thickly planted with ground cover. However, healthy well-grown plants should not normally need such a life-saving technique.

PRUNING AND DIVISION

Keeping the plants tidy is an occasional job which will be needed for certain plants – those that are very vigorous and have to be restrained from swamping other plants, and those that become straggly after several years and require cutting back to keep them compact, such as ericas. The removal of dead twigs and old flowering stems is also part of regular pruning. With some woody plants pruning may be necessary in the early years after planting to encourage branching near ground level. (See also the Wisley Handbook, *Pruning Ornamental Shrubs.*)

Herbaceous plants like *Alchemilla mollis*, hostas and daylilies may become overcrowded and should be divided after about four to five years.

A Selection of Plants

This chapter contains information on plants suitable for ground cover. These are divided into the four main categories outlined on pp.203–4 and are listed alphabetically by their botanical name within each group.

In most cases, the name of the species or hybrid group is used for the heading, and its approximate height and the planting distance are given at the end of each entry. The height is that of the plant when not in flower; the planting distance is that recommended in order to obtain 75 to 100 per cent cover within one to two years. Both may vary to some extent according to the climate, soil and other factors. Details of soil, aspect or any special requirements are included and varieties, cultivars or similar species are also mentioned where appropriate. The plant is described as deciduous or evergreen according to whether it loses or keeps its leaves in winter.

GROUP A

Evergreens of rapid growth and high density cover which either carpet the ground with spreading stems, rooting as they go, or colonise by means of underground shoots, suckers, or stolons. The most efficient ground covers, making a complete canopy in the first year after planting. All are very tolerant of shade and undemanding in their soil requirements.

Galeobdolon

G. argentatum (Lamium galeobdolon 'Variegatum'), yellow archangel. Perennial carpeter of tremendous vigour with marbled green and white foliage and yellow flowers in early summer. Excellent under trees and shrubs, but avoid areas where small plants might be smothered. Height 6–9 in. (15–23 cm). Planting distance 24–36 in. (60–90 cm).

Hedera (ivy)

Carpeting or climbing shrubs for almost any situation from dense shade to full sun.
H. canariensis 'Azorica'. Large matt-green leaves. 'Gloire de Marengo' ('Variegata') has foliage marked white, grey and green

212

The robust Irish ivy, *Hedera helix* 'Hibernica', is especially useful
beneath trees, where not even grass would grow, and thrives in almost
any conditions

---

but is less reliable in cold gardens. Height 6–9 in. (15–23 cm).
Planting distance 36–48 in. (90–120 cm).
H. colchica. Thick dark green leaves. 'Dentata' has paler larger
leaves. 'Dentata Variegata' has foliage margined creamy yellow.
'Sulphur Heart' ('Paddy's Pride') has a central splash of gold on
the leaves. Height 6–9 in. (15–23 cm). Planting distance 36–48 in.
(90–120 cm).
H. helix, common ivy. Extremely variable and adaptable, first-
class ground cover. 'Hibernica', Irish ivy, with large dark green
leaves, is particularly vigorous, dense and fast-growing. Many
other forms, with green or variegated foliage, are suitable,
including 'Green Ripple' and 'Goldheart'. Height 6—12 in.
(15–30 cm). Planting distance, depending on vigour, 24–48 in.
(60–120 cm).

Hypericum (see also p.222)

H. calycinum, rose of Sharon. Colonising shrub with saucer-
shaped golden yellow flowers from summer into autumn. Sun or
shade in any well-drained soil. Cut to near ground level each April
for densest cover. Height 9–12 in. (23–30 cm). Planting distance
15–18 in. (38–46 cm). (See p.198.)

Waldsteinia ternata makes a pretty evergreen carpet in sun or shade, bearing golden yellow flowers in April and May

---

Vinca (periwinkle)

Carpeting, trailing shrubs.

V. major. Blue or white flowers in spring. Ideal for almost any position and soil, except poorly drained, and less dense on very dry exposed sites. Requires initial weeding. Cut back hard after flowering when untidy. 'Variegata' has leaves blotched and edged creamy white. Subsp. *hirsuta* is very vigorous, eventually forming dense rampant cover. Height 6–9 in. (15–23 cm). Planting distance 18–24 in. (46–60 cm).

V. minor. Smaller leaves but very effective in similar conditions. Forms with variegated foliage and single or double flowers in white, blue or purple. All are useful and attractive. Height 4–6 in. (10–15 cm). Planting distance 15–18 in. (38–46 cm). (See p.194.)

Waldsteinia

W. ternata. Perennial carpeter making mats of dark green lobed leaves, with yellow flowers in spring. Excellent cover in any situation and soil. Height 3–4 in. (8–10 cm). Planting distance 12 in. (30 cm).

GROUP B

Evergreens, unless otherwise stated, of medium to slow growth and high to medium density cover. They may be hummock-forming, with a central low stem and many widespreading branches; or carpeting, with rooting prostrate stems; or colonising by spreading underground. They take two seasons to cover the ground, but in time achieve a dense network of branches.

Alyssum

A. saxatilis (*Aurinia saxatilis*), gold dust. Perennial hummock-former with grey-green leaves and masses of bright yellow flowers in spring. 'Citrinum' has paler flowers. Sun and well-drained soil. Height 9 in. (23 cm). Planting distance 15 in. (38 cm).

Anthemis (see also p.235)

A. cupaniana. Hummock-forming perennial with feathery silver foliage and white daisy flowers in late spring. Sun and well-drained soil. Dislikes wet. Height 9 in. (23 cm). Planting distance 18–24 in. (46–60 cm).

Arabis

A. albida (*A. caucasica*). Perennial hummock-former with greyish green leaves and white flowers in spring. Does not succeed in poorly drained soil and becomes straggly in shade. 'Flore Pleno' has double flowers. 'Variegata' has cream-edged foliage. Height 5 in. (13 cm). Planting distance 9—15 in. (23–28 cm).

Arctostaphylos

A. uva-ursi, bearberry. Carpeting shrub with dark green leaves and tiny white or pink flowers in April, followed by small red berries. Acid soil in light or dappled shade. Height 6 in. (15 cm). Planting distance 15 in. (38 cm). (See p.216).

Asarum

A. europaeum. Perennial carpeter with glossy dark green rounded leaves. Useful in shade but not for very dry positions. *A. canadense* and *A. shuttleworthii* are less dense. Height 3–4 in. (8–10 cm). Planting distance 9–12 in. (23–30 cm).

Aubrieta

A. deltoidea. Hummock-forming perennial with small grey-green leaves and flowers ranging from purple to pink, in spring. Sun

The bearberry, *Arctostaphylos uva-ursi*, gives year-round interest with flowers, berries and foliage

and well-drained soil. Cut back after flowering when it becomes straggly. Height 3–4 in. (7–10 cm). Planting distance 12 in. (30 cm).

Ballota

B. pseudodictamnus. Hummock-forming woody-based perennial with woolly grey-white rounded leaves. Sun and dry position. Cut back old growth to main rosette in spring. Height 9 in. (23 cm). Planting distance 15 in. (38 cm).

Calluna (heather)

C. vulgaris. Hummock-forming shrub with numerous forms, varying in colour of foliage (some valuable in winter) and of flowers, from white to purple, produced in summer, autumn or early winter. Acid soil. Happier in sun, though tolerant of slight shade. Clip over in spring to maintain compact habit. Height 6–18 in. (15–46 cm). Planting distance 9–18 cm. (23–46 cm). (See p.201.)

Ceanothus

C. thyrsiflorus var. *repens*. Hummock-forming shrub with glossy green leaves and pale blue flowers in early summer. Full sun. Good for banks. Height and planting distance 36 in. (90 cm). (See p.200.)

216

Left: The ever-popular aubrieta, in this case A. *deltoidea* 'Red Carpet', succeeds in any dry sunny situation
Right: *Convolvulus cneorum* needs a sheltered position but is easily increased from cuttings, which should be taken in summer and placed in gentle heat

Cerastium

C. tomentosum, snow in summer. Carpeting and colonising perennial with silvery grey leaves and white flowers in summer. Full sun. Invasive when established but useful in dry situations. Height 6 in. (15 cm). Planting distance 15 in. (38 cm).

Cistus (rock rose)

C. parviflorus. Hummock-forming shrub with grey-green felted foliage and clear pink flowers in summer. Full sun. *C. salviifolius* 'Prostratus' and *C. lusitanicus* are also good ground covers but less hardy. Height 18–24 in. (46–60 cm). Planting distance 24–30 in. (60–75 cm).

Convolvulus

C. cneorum. Hummock-forming shrub with silvery leaves and white pink-flushed trumpet flowers in summer. Full sun and well-drained soil. Not successful in cold districts. Height 18–24 in. (46–60 cm). Planting distance 24 in. (60 cm).

Cotoneaster (see also p.238)

Shrubs suitable for any soil and position except dense shade.
C. congestus. Carpeter with dull green leaves, small pinkish white flowers in spring and bright red berries. Very dense and compact, though of relatively slow growth. Height 3–4 in. (8–10 cm). Planting distance 12 in. (30 cm).
C. conspicuus. Hummock-forming, with shining dark green leaves, numerous white flowers in early summer and long-lasting scarlet berries. 'Decorus' is more horizontal and spreading, making large dense mounds. Excellent for banks. Height 72 in. (180 cm). Planting distance 60–72 in. (150–180 cm).
C. salicifolius. 'Gnom' is the best of several named forms, a prostrate carpeter with neat foliage and small red fruits in autumn. Grows rapidly to give dense cover. Height 3–4 in. (8–10 cm). Planting distance 18–24 in. (46–60 cm).

Cytisus (broom)

Hummock-forming deciduous shrubs needing full sun and well-drained soil. Slender green twigs give evergreen effect.
C. × kewensis. Downy leaves and creamy white or pale yellow pea flowers in May. Height 12 in. (30 cm). Planting distance 24 in. (60 cm).
C. scoparius var. *prostratus*. Silky-hairy leaves and young twigs and rich yellow flowers in May. Variety of common broom. Growth medium to rapid but weeding necessary in first year. Height 12–15 in. (30–38 cm). Planting distance 36 in. (90 cm).

Daboecia

D. cantabrica, Irish heath. Hummock-forming shrub with sprays of bell-shaped flowers, purple to white depending on form, in summer and autumn. 'Atropurpurea' is vigorous with deep rose-purple flowers. *D. azorica* has rich crimson flowers but is less hardy. Acid soil and sun. Height and planting distance 15–18 in. (38–46 cm).

Dianthus

Garden pinks. Hummock-forming perennials with flowers varying from white to pink to crimson, often scented, in summer. 'Mrs Sinkins', 'Dad's Favourite' and many other forms are suitable. Full sun, alkaline soil. Height 9 in. (23 cm). Planting distance 9–12 in. (23–30 cm).

Euonymus fortunei 'Emerald Gaiety' may develop a more upright habit than other cultivars

Dryas

D. octopetala, mountain avens. Carpeting shrub with small oak-like leaves and white dog-rose flowers in early summer, followed by fluffy seedheeds. Slow-growing at first then forming a dense mat. Full sun. Height 2–3 in. (5–8 cm). Planting distance 12–15 in. (30–38 cm).

Erica (heath)

E. herbacea (*E. carnea*). Hummock-forming or carpeting shrub, with numerous forms in a range of foliage colours and bearing pink or white flowers, mainly in winter. 'Springwood White' and 'Springwood Pink' are spreading and particularly effective. Best in an open position on acid or slightly alkaline soil rich in leaf-mould. May be clipped in spring for denser growth. Other species and hybrids like *E. vagans* and *E. × darleyensis* are also good. Height 9 in. (23 cm). Planting distance 15 in. (38 cm).

Euonymus

E. fortunei var. *radicans*. Carpeting or climbing shrub with oval shining green leaves. Makes dense cover in sun or shade. 'Kewensis' is a miniature version with smaller leaves. Other forms, such as 'Emerald and Gold' and 'Emerald Gaiety', with variegated foliage, and 'Coloratus', with leaves turning purple in autumn, can also be used. Height 9 in. (23 cm). Planting distance 12–18 in. (30–46 cm).

E. fortunei f. *carrieri*. Hummock-forming shrub, low and spreading, with small pale green flowers in summer, followed by fruits. Height 24 in. (60 cm). Planting distance 30 in. (75 cm).

× *Gaulnettya*

× *G.* 'Wisley Pearl'. Evergreen colonising shrub with bushy habit and neat foliage, white flowers in early summer and purplish red berries. Hybrid of *Gaultheria* and *Pernettya*. Acid soil with leaf-mould, tolerant of shade. Height 24–36 in. (60–90 cm). Planting distance 24 in. (60 cm).

Genista (broom)

Deciduous shrubs related to *Cytisus* (p.218), requiring a sunny position and well-drained soil. Yellow flowers in May and June.
G. hispanica, Spanish gorse. Hummock-forming, with the crowded twigs and spines giving an evergreen appearance. Height and planting distance 24 in. (60 cm).
G. lydia. More pendulous hummock-forming growth, with grey-green twigs. Height 12–15 in. (30–38 cm). Planting distance 18–21 in. (46–54 cm).
G. pilosa. Carpeter forming a low tangled mass. 'Procumbens' is a prostrate form. Useful on banks and will succeed in light shade. Height 12 in. (30 cm). Planting distance 15–18 in. (38–46 cm).
G. sagittalis. Hummock-forming, sometimes carpeting, with an evergreen effect from the green winged stems. Gives dense cover once established. *G. delphinensis* is like a miniature version. Height 9–12 in. (23–30 cm). Planting distance 12–15 in. (30–38 cm).

× *Halimiocistus*

× *H. sahucii*. Hummock-forming shrub with a profusion of white flowers throughout summer. Natural hybrid of *Cistus* and *Halimium*. Full sun and good drainage. Hardy in all but coldest areas. Height 12 in. (30 cm). Planting distance 21–24 in. (54–60 cm).

Halimium

H. lasianthum. Hummock-forming shrub with greyish leaves and rich yellow flowers with or without a dark central blotch in May. Full sun and well-drained soil. May be damaged in severe winters. Height 12 in. (30 cm). Planting distance 18–24 in. (46–60 cm).

Above: The graceful *Genista lydia* is sometimes hit by late frosts
Below: × *Halimiocistus sahucii*, a dwarf shrub of spreading but close growth

Hebe (see also p.240)

Shrubs for sunny well-drained situations.

H. albicans. Hummock-forming, with grey foliage and spikes of white flowers in summer. 'Pewter Dome' is a fine form with narrower leaves. Height 12 in. (30 cm). Planting distance 18–24 in. (46–60 cm).

H. pinguifolia 'Pagei'. Hummock-forming, occasionally carpeting, with blue-grey foliage and clustered white flowers in May, sometimes repeated in late summer. May die out in centre and requires trimming in April to encourage re-growth. Height 6–9 in. (15–23 cm). Planting distance 15 in. (38 cm).

H. rakaiensis. Hummock-forming, making compact mounds of light green foliage, with white flowers in June and July. *H. vernicosa* is similar, with darker 'varnished' leaves. Height 18–24 in. (46–60 cm). Planting distance 21–24 in. (54–60 cm). (See p.207.)

Helianthemum (sun rose)

Hummock-forming shrubs needing full sun and good drainage. Cut back after flowering

H. nummularium 'Amy Baring'. Green leaves and deep yellow flowers in summer. Forms dense spreading mats. Height 4–6 in. (10–15 cm). Planting distance 12–18 in. (30–46 cm). (see p.19.)

Garden hybrids. Green or grey foliage and single or double flowers in many colours. 'Wisley Pink' and 'Wisley Primrose' are dense grey-leaved forms. Ideal for a sunny bank. Height 6–9 in. (15–23 cm). Planting distance 12–18 in. (30–46 cm).

Hypericum (see also p.213)

H. cerastoides. Carpeting shrub with greyish hairy leaves and bright yellow flowers in May. Full sun and well-drained soil. Height 3 in. (8 cm). Planting distance 9–12 in. (23–30 cm).

H. × moserianum. Hummock-forming, slightly colonising shrub with large golden yellow flowers from July to October. Stands some shade but prefers sun. Often killed back in winter. Height 18 in. (46 cm). Planting distance 18–21 in. (46–54 cm).

Iberis (candytuft)

I. sempervirens. Hummock-forming shrub with narrow dark green leaves and plentiful white flowers from April to June. 'Snowflake' is a compact form. Sunny well-drained spot. Height 9–12 in. (23–30 cm). Planting distance 12–15 in. (30–38 cm). (See p.249.)

Above: The delightful *Hebe pinguifolia* 'Pagei' forms a low mat of blue-grey foliage
Below: The pale pink orange-centred flowers of *Helianthemum* 'Wisley pink' are borne from late May to the end of June

The prostrate *Juniperus communis* 'Depressa Aurea' becomes golden yellow in summer, particularly when planted in full sun, and bronze in autumn

---

Juniperus (juniper)

Hummock-forming shrubs, sometimes carpeting or rooting down. Particularly useful on poor soils, including chalk, and in hot dry situations.

J. communis var. *jackii*. Sea-green foliage and low spreading branches. Open sunny position. Subsp. *depressa* and other forms like 'Depressa Aurea', 'Dumosa', 'Effusa' and 'Repanda', with variously coloured foliage, are equally useful. Height 6–9 in. (15–23 cm). Planting distance 24 in. (60 cm).

J. conferta. Bright green prickly leaves and prostrate habit. Tolerates some shade. Height 6–9 in. (15–23 cm). Planting distance 24 in. (60 cm).

J. horizontalis. Available in several forms with blue-grey, bronze or green foliage. Makes thick creeping mats eventually but requires weeding in early years. Sun. Height 6 in. (15 cm). Planting distance 18–24 in. (46–60 cm).

J. × *media* 'Pfitzeriana'. Green and grey-green leaves on wide-spreading arching branches. Will withstand dense shade of trees. Forms with golden foliage are less vigorous. Height 36 in. (90 cm). Planting distance 48–72 in. (1.2–1.8 m).

J. sabina var. *tamariscifolia*. Bright green leaves on closely tiered branches. Dense cover, though relatively slow. Accepts partial shade. Height 15–18 in. (38–46 cm). Planting distance 24–30 in. (60–75 cm).

Leucothoe

L. fontanesiana. Carpeting shrub with leathery green leaves turning bronze in autumn and clusters of white flowers along arching branches in May. Acid leafy soil and shade. Height 36 in. (90 cm). Planting distance 30–36 in. (75–90 cm).

Lithospermum

L. diffusum (*Lithodora diffusa*). Hummock-forming, trailing shrub with vivid blue flowers in early summer. 'Heavenly Blue' and 'Grace Ward' have larger flowers. Acid soil. Will grow in some shade but best in a sunny open position. Tends to die out in patches. Height 9 in. (23 cm). Planting distance 12–15 in. (30–38 cm).

Lonicera (honeysuckle) (see also p.247)

L. pileata. Hummock-forming, sometimes carpeting shrub with neat glossy dark green foliage, occasionally producing clusters of translucent violet berries. Any well-drained soil in sun or shade. The related *L. nitida* 'Graziosa' is similar. Height 18 in. (46 cm). Planting distance 24–30 in. (60–75 cm).

Lithospermum diffusum 'Heavenly Blue' should be lightly trimmed after flowering

Mahonia

M. aquifolium. Colonising shrub with polished dark green pinnate leaves, golden yellow flowers in early spring and blue-black berries. Succeeds in shade and dry soil if mulched annually. Cut back in April each year to encourage dense habit. *M. repens* var. *rotundifolia* is taller and gives equally dense cover when mature, though both may be slow to establish. Height and planting distance 24 in. (60 cm).

Osteospermum

O. jucundum (*Dimorphotheca barberiae*). Hummock-forming shrubby perennial with slender light green leaves and mauve-pink daisy flowers throughout summer. 'Compactum' is mat-forming and particularly suitable. 'Nairobi Purple' has deep purple flowers but is less hardy. Excellent summer cover in sunny well-drained site. Not for cold wet districts. Height 6–9 in. (15–23 cm). Planting distance 15–18 in. (38–46 cm).

Pachysandra

P. terminalis. Carpeting shrub with diamond-shaped leaves at ends of the stems and spikes of greenish flowers in spring. Very useful in shade. 'Variegata', with white-striped leaves, is slightly less vigorous. Height 3–4 in. (8–10 cm). Planting distance 9–12 in. (23–30 cm).

Parahebe

P. catarractae. Hummock-forming deciduous shrub with white or blue-purple flowers in late summer. Open sunny position in well-drained soil. *P. lyallii* is similar, with smaller foliage and more prostrate, often carpeting. Height 9 in. (23 cm). Planting distance 12 in. (30 cm).

Pernettya

Colonising shrubs forming dense thickets. Acid soil and full sun. *P. mucronata.* Wiry thickly leafy stems and numerous white heather-like flowers in May and June, followed by variously coloured berries lasting through winter. Several forms available. Should be planted in groups, including a male form, to ensure berries. Height 24–36 in. (60–90 cm). Planting distance 24 in. (60 cm).

Left: *Pachysandra terminalis* 'Variegata' flourishes in any moist soil
Right: The variable *Parahebe catarractae* makes effective ground cover in sun

P. prostrata subsp. *pentlandii*. Dense dark glossy green leaves, white flowers in early summer and black berries. Spreading growth and tolerant of slight shade. Height 12–18 in. (30–46 cm). Planting distance 15 in. (38 cm).

Phlomis

P. fruticosa, Jerusalem sage. Hummock-forming shrub with woolly grey-green foliage and whorls of bright yellow flowers in summer. Gives dense cover in a sunny sheltered position and best in warm areas. *P. chrysophylla* differs in its lower habit and golden green foliage. Both ideal for a dry sunny bank. Height 36 in. (90 cm). Planting distance 30–36 in. (75–90 cm).

Potentilla (see also p.242)

P. fruticosa, shrubby cinquefoil. Hummock-forming deciduous shrub with small divided leaves and yellow flowers from early summer to autumn. Represented in gardens by numerous hybrids, many of spreading dense habit, such as 'Longacre', 'Elizabeth' and 'Gold Drop'. *P. davurica* var. *mandshurica* has grey-green leaves and white flowers. Open sunny position in any reasonably drained soil. Height 15–18 in. (38–46 cm). Planting distance 24–30 in. (60–75 cm).

Left: The gold- and purple-leaved forms of common sage, *Salvia officinalis*, go well together
Right: The well-known *Senecio* 'Sunshine' is a good shrubby ground cover for seaside gardens

---

Prunus

P. laurocerasus 'Otto Luyken' Hummock-forming shrub with narrow glossy green leaves and small white flowers in April. A low compact form of cherry laurel. The spreading 'Zabeliana' and 'Schipkaensis' are equally good ground cover, tolerant of dense shade, even from trees, and almost any soil. Height 36 in. (90 cm). Planting distance 36–48 in. (90–120 cm).

Salvia

S. officinalis, common sage. Hummock-forming shrub with soft grey green aromatic leaves and purple flowers in summer. Full sun and well-drained soil. May suffer in harsh winters. Can be trimmed in late spring to keep compact. 'Purpurascens' and 'Icterina', purple and golden sage, are slightly less vigorous. Height 12–18 in. (30–46 cm). Planting distance 18–24 in. (46–60 cm).

Senecio

S. 'Sunshine'. Hummock-forming shrub with grey foliage and yellow daisy flowers in summer. Sun and good drainage. Height 36 in. (90 cm). Planting distance 36–48 in. (90–120 cm).

GROUP C

Deciduous, unless otherwise stated, herbaceous perennials of medium to slow growth and high to medium density cover, forming clumps as the roots gradually increase. Relatively slow but steady ground covers, providing a thick canopy of leaves, especially in summer.

Acanthus

A. *mollis* var. *latifolius*, bear's breeches. Bold rich green leaves and tall mauve flower spikes in summer. Prefers sun but will tolerate shade. Spreads from suckers and can be invasive. Height and planting distance 36 in. (90 cm).

Alchemilla

A. *mollis*, lady's mantle. Fresh green wavy-edged leaves and frothy yellow-green flowers in summer. Succeeds in sun or shade and any soil. Cut off flowers to prevent seeding and divide if necessary after about five years. Height 6–9 in. (15–23 cm). Planting distance 15–18 in. (38–46 cm). (See p.231.)

Bergenia

Species and hybrids. Large evergreen foliage, often changing colour in winter, and heads of purple to pink flowers in spring. Any situation and soil, though more straggling in deep shade. Increasing from creeping rhizomes. Avoid B. *ciliata* and B. 'Ballawley', which can be damaged by frost and wind. Height 5–12 in. (13–30 cm). Planting distance 9–24 in. (23–60 cm).

Brunnera

B. *macrophylla*. Big cabbagey leaves and blue forget-me-not flowers in spring. Best in shade as foliage is liable to scorch in sun. Height 12 in. (30 cm). Planting distance 15–18 in. (38–46 cm).

Geranium (cranesbill) (see also p.239)

Versatile and dense ground covers with attractive foliage and flowers, mostly produced in summer. Thriving in any reasonable soil and positions ranging from full sun to deep shade.
G. *endressi*. Divided light green leaves and continuous pink flowers. 'Wargrave Pink' has brighter pink flowers. The hybrid 'Claridge

Druce' is even more vigorous, with magenta-pink flowers. Both spread from the central rosette and retain old foliage in winter. Height 12–21 in. (30–54 cm). Planting distance 12–15 in. (30–38 cm).
G. himalayense. Dark green leaves and violet-blue flowers. Spreads from suckers. The hybrid 'Johnson's Blue' has paler blue flowers. Height 9–12 in. (23–30 cm). Planting distance 12–15 in. (30–38 cm).
G. × magnificum. Hairy leaves, often tinted in autumn, and violet-blue flowers. Withstands hot sun. G. ibericum and G. platypetalum are similar. Height 9–12 in. (23–30 cm). Planting distance 12–15 in. (30–38 cm).
G. phaeum, mourning widow. Maroon to white flowers in late spring. Excellent in deep shade, as are G. punctatum, with mauve-purple flowers, and G. nodosum, with a succession of small lilac flowers above glossy green leaves. Height 12 in. (30 cm). Planting distance 15–18 in. (38–46 cm).
G. psilostemon. Deeply cut leaves and bright magenta flowers with dark centres. Best in open position. Height 30 in. (75 cm). Planting distance 24–36 in. (60–90 cm).
G. sanguineum. Dark green leaves and plentiful flowers of deep magenta to white. Prefers some sun. Subsp. lancastriense is more prostrate with pink veined flowers. Spreading by suckers. Height 6–9 in. (15–23 cm). Planting distance 12–15 in. (30–38 cm).
G. sylvaticum. White, pink or lavender-blue flowers in May. Seeds freely. Very tolerant of shade. Height 12–15 in. (30–38 cm). Planting distance 15–18 in. (38–46 cm).

Geum

G. 'Borisii'. Rich green hairy leaves in a dense mound and bright orange flowers in early summer. Sun and any soil. Height 6–9 in. (15–23 cm). Planting distance 12 in. (30 cm). (See p.232.)

Hemerocallis (daylily)

Species and garden hybrids. Arching grassy foliage giving dense summer cover and lily flowers in a range of colours, especially yellows, in summer. Sun or partial shade in any soil. Most form compact clumps, but H. flava and H. fulva have running roots which can be invasive. Height 18–24 in. (46–60 cm). Planting distance 18 in. (46 cm). (See p.211.)

Hosta

Indispensable foliage plants for dense shade, doing equally well

Above: The charming lady's mantle, *Alchemilla mollis*, will proliferate in almost any situation
Below: *Geranium* × *magnificum*, often known by the name of one of its parents, *G. ibericum*

Geum 'Borisii' forms dense clumps which should be divided every few years to keep it healthy

in sun and not fussy about soil. Thick summer cover. Lily-shaped flowers, generally lilac-coloured, in summer.

H. crispula. Long pointed spreading leaves margined white. Height 12 in. (30 cm). Planting distance 15–18 in. (38–46 cm).

H. decorata. Blunt broad leaves edged in white. Like most hostas, should be divided after five years rather than ten. Height 9–12 in. (23–30 cm). Planting distances 15 in. (38 cm).

H. fortunei. 'Albopicta' and 'Obscura Marginata' have yellow-margined leaves. 'Hyacintha' has blue-green leaves. 'Obscura' has handsome green leaves. *H. fortunei* f. *rugosa* has corrugated leaves. Height and planting distance 18 in. (46 cm).

H. plantaginea. Pale green glossy arching foliage and scented white trumpet flowers in late summer. Flowers best in warm moist situation. Height and planting distance 15 in. (38 cm).

H. rectifolia 'Tall Boy'. Long pointed leaves and notable lilac flowers. Vigorous growth. Height and planting distance 18 in. (46 cm). (See p.249.)

H. sieboldiana. Huge grey-green leaves, blue-grey and crinkled in var. *elegans*, yellow-margined in 'Frances Williams'. Height 18 in. (46 cm). Planting distance 18–24 in. (46–60 cm).

H. undulata var. *erromena*. Long glossy green leaves and tall spikes of purple flowers. Var. *undulata* and var. *univittata* have smaller variegated foliage and are less dense. Height and planting distance 18 in. (46 cm). (See p.202.)

H. ventricosa. Dark shining green leaves and rich violet-purple flowers. 'Variegata' and 'Aureomaculata' are good variegated forms but slightly less vigorous. Height 15 in. (38 cm). Planting distance 18 in. (46 cm).

Iris

I. foetidissima. Dark green arching evergreen foliage, with insignificant flowers followed by orange seed pods in autumn. Thrives in any position unless badly drained, including deep shade and dry soil. Spreads from rhizomes. 'Citrina' has larger pale yellow flowers in early summer and good pods of red berries. Height 18 in. (46 cm). Planting distance 12–15 in. (30–38 cm).

Liriope

L. muscari. Grass-like evergreen leaves and spikes of lavender flowers in autumn. Sunny dry situation. Height 9 in. (23 cm). Planting distance 9–12 in. (23–30 cm). (See p.234.)

Nepeta

N. × *faassenii*, catmint. Small greyish leaves and sprays of lavender flowers throughout summer. Prefers full sun and good drainage and less hardy in cold damp districts. Cut back old growths in spring. Height 9 in. (23 cm). Planting distance 12 in. (30 cm).

Origanum

O. vulgare 'Aureum'. Bright golden yellow foliage developing in spring to give good summer cover. Needs open well-drained site. *O. vulgare*, wild marjoram, has dark green leaves and tiny mauve flowers in summer. Height 6 in. (15 cm). Planting distance 12 in. (30 cm).

Pachyphragma

P. macrophyllum. Rounded glossy bright green leaves and white flowers in May. Likes shade in fairly moist soil. Height 6–9 in. (15–23 cm). Planting distance 12–15 in. (30–38 cm).

Left: *Liriope muscari* has arching shiny leaves and flowers most freely in sun
Right: The red bells of *Pulmonaria rubra* appear at the end of January and continue until March

---

Polygonum (knotweed) (see also p.242)

P. campanulatum. Winter rosettes form widespreading trails of soft green foliage, with long-lasting pink flowers in summer. Spreads rapidly from creeping roots but not invasive. Prefers moist soil and is content with some shade. Height and planting distance 18–24 in. (46–60 cm).

Pulmonaria (lungwort)

Species and hybrids. Almost all are effective easy ground covers for sun or shade, preferably in moist soil. Spreading by roots and also from seed. They flower in early spring. Height 5–6 in. (13–15 cm). Planting distance 12 in. (30 cm).
P. angustifolia. Bristly leaves and blue flowers. 'Mawson's Variety' and 'Azurea' are good forms. (See p.210.)
P. officinalis, spotted dog. Evergreen leaves spotted and blotched with white and pink flowers turning blue. *P. saccharata* is similar.
P. rubra. Evergreen leaves and early red flowers.

GROUP D

Deciduous or evergreen plants of rapid to medium growth and high to medium density cover, either carpeters which root on the surface, or colonisers which spread underground. Most cover the ground quickly, but make thinner growth initially than other groups and need two seasons to achieve a dense canopy.

234

Acaena

A. *novae-zelandiae*. Deciduous carpeting perennial with rounded hairy leaves and inconspicuous purplish flower heads in summer. Roots at the nodes. Sun and well-drained soil. Other species like A. *caesiiglauca* are also effective but variable in density of cover. Height 3–4 in. (8–10 cm). Planting distance 15–28 in. (38–70 cm).

Ajuga

A. *reptans*, bugle. Evergreen perennial carpeter with dark green leaves and spikes of blue flowers in spring. 'Atropurpurea', with glossy reddish purple foliage, and 'Multicolor', with purple, pink, cream and bronze foliage, colour best in sun. 'Jungle Beauty' is a large green-leaved vigorous form. Sun or partial shade and moist soil. Needs good conditions to avoid becoming bare in the centre and requires feeding. Height 2–5 in. (5–13 cm). Planting distance 9–15 in. (23–38 cm).

Antennaria

A. *dioica*. Evergreen carpeting perennial with greyish leaves and small white flowers in summer. Sun and well drained soil. Will form a close mat but is somewhat slow-growing and needs weeding in first year. Height 1–2 in. (2–5 cm). Planting distance 9 in. (23 cm).

Anthemis (see also p.215)

A. *nobilis* (*Chamaemelum nobile*), chamomile. Evergreen perennial carpeter with feathery leaves and white daisy flowers in summer, both aromatic. Sun and light or sandy soil. Apt to die out in patches but gaps can be filled with young plants. A useful alternative to grass and may be mown in the same way. 'Treneague', which is non-flowering and has dense mossy foliage, is best for a lawn. Height 1–3 in. (2–8 cm). Planting distance 9–15 in. (23–38 cm). (See p.236)

Artemisia

A. *canescens* (of gardens). Evergreen colonising perennial with silver-grey filigree foliage. Full sun or growth will be sparse. A. *stelleriana*, dusty miller, has broad divided grey-white downy leaves. Height 9–12 in. (23–30 cm). Planting distance 15–18 in. (38–46 cm). (See p.236)

Above: *Anthemis nobilis* 'Treneague' (left) makes a lovely scented lawn or clothing for a bank; the striking *Artemisia canescens* (right) is happy in any ordinary soil
Below: The native hard fern, *Blechnum spicant* (left), prefers lime-free soil; *Centaurea* 'John Coutts' (right) appreciates a well-drained position

Arundinaria (bamboo)

A. viridistriata. Evergreen coloniser with leaves of dark green striped with rich yellow. Spreads from creeping rhizome and may be less dense at edges of clump. Succeeds in sun or moderate shade. Height and planting distance 24 in. (60 cm).

Asperula

A. odorata (*Galium odoratum*), sweet woodruff. Deciduous colonising perennial quickly making dense drifts of rich green foliage, with scented white flowers in May. Thrives in shade and can be invasive. Height 4–5 in. (10–13 cm). Planting distance 24 in. (60 cm).

Blechnum

B. spicant, hard fern. Evergreen colonising fern with dark green ladder-like fronds. Prefers moist leafy soil, lime-free. Relatively slow growth but useful in shade of trees and shrubs. Height 9–15 in. (23–38 cm). Planting distance 12 in. (30 cm).

Campanula (bellflower)

Colonising perennials with blue flowers in summer. Will accept some shade but better in sun, in well-drained soil.
C. portenschlagiana. Deciduous, with clusters of blue-purple bell-shaped flowers. Height 3–4 in. (8–10 cm). Planting distance 9–12 in. (23–30 cm).
C. poscharskyana. Dense evergreen leaves and trailing stems with starry lilac-blue flowers. Can be invasive. 'E.K. Toogood' is less rampant. Height 3–4 in. (8–10 cm).

Centaurea

C. 'John Coutts'. Deciduous perennial coloniser with grey foliage and pink knapweed flowers in early summer. Full sun. Height 6 in. (15 cm). Planting distance 12–15 in. (30–38 cm).

Ceratostigma

C. plumbaginoides. Deciduous colonising perennial with leaves becoming red-tinted in autumn at the same time as the dark blue flower heads appear. Sun in well-drained soil. Height 9 in. (23 cm). Planting distance 12–15 in. (30–38 cm). (See p.239)

Cornus

C. canadensis, creeping dogwood. Deciduous perennial coloniser with leaves often changing colour in autumn and white four-bracted flowers in summer. Spreads by underground shoots. Acid moist soil and partial shade. Height 4–6 in. (10–15 cm). Planting distance 12–15 in. (30–38 cm).

Cotoneaster (see also p.218)

C. dammeri. Evergreen carpeting shrub with slender creeping stems and coral-red berries in autumn. Spreading thin growth at first, later dense, but needs weeding for first two years. Almost any soil and situation. 'Coral Beauty' is less ground-hugging. Height 3–4 in. (8–10 cm). Planting distance 24 in. (60 cm). (See p.202)

Cotula

C. squalida. Evergreen carpeting perennial with ferny bronze-green leaves and creamy yellow button flowers in summer. Makes a mat of foliage in dry or damp soil, sun or shade, and is fairly invasive. Height 1 in. (2 cm). Planting distance 9 in. (23 cm).

Dicentra

D. formosa. Deciduous perennial coloniser with light green ferny leaves and mauve-pink locket flowers in late spring. Shade and moist soil. Height 9 in. (23 cm). Planting distance 15 in. (38 cm).

Duchesnea

D. indica (*Fragaria indica*). Deciduous carpeting perennial with dark green strawberry-like foliage, yellow flowers in spring and red fruits. Only for rougher positions where it cannot smother smaller plants. Height 3 in. (8 cm). Planting distance 15 in. (38 cm).

Epimedium

Colonising perennials with lobed leaves, often attractively tinted in spring and autumn, and variously coloured flowers in spring. Excellent in sun or shade and any soil, but relatively slow.
E. perralderianum. Evergreen, with large shining green leaves and bright yellow flowers. *E. pinnatum* var. *colchicum* and *E. × perralchicum* are similar. Height and planting distance 12 in. (30 cm).

Left: *Ceratostigma plumbaginoides* flowers continuously in September and October
Right: The foliage of *Epimedium × rubrum* is handsomely tinted when young, later turning pale green

---

E. × versicolor. Deciduous, with coppery leaves in spring and pink flowers. 'Sulphureum' has yellow flowers and is more vigorous. *E. × rubrum*, with crimson flowers, is equally good. Cut off old leaf stalks in spring. Height and planting distance 9 in. (23 cm).

Euphorbia (spurge)

E. robbiae. Evergreen perennial coloniser with rosettes of dark green leaves and tall spires of greenish flowers in spring. Sometimes slow to establish but then spreads freely by underground runners. Sun or shade in any soil. Height 15 in. (38 cm). Planting distance 18 in. (46 cm).

Gaultheria

G. procumbens, creeping wintergreen. Evergreen colonising shrub with leathery glossy leaves, aromatic and turning reddish in autumn, tiny pinkish white flowers in July and August and vivid red berries. Acid soil in shade. Happy in dry conditions once established. Height 6 in. (15 cm). Planting distance 12–15 in. (30–38 cm).

Geranium (cranesbill) (see also p.229)

Deciduous carpeting perennials with rounded divided leaves and saucer-shaped flowers. Tolerant of many situations and soils.

Left: *Geranium* 'Russell Prichard' is valuable for its very long flowering season

---

G. macrorrhizum. Light green aromatic leaves, changing colour in autumn, and magenta, pink or white flowers according to the form in late spring. Extremely dense cover. Height 9–12 in. (23–30 cm). Planting distance 12–15 in. (30–38 cm).
G. 'Russell Prichard'. Greyish green leaves and continuous pink flowers from July onwards. Sends out dense trails of foliage in summer, dying back to the rootstock in winter. Requires full sun and good drainage, and may be slightly tender in cold areas. *G. wallichianum* has a similar habit, is hardy and does not mind shade. 'Buxton's Variety' has blue flowers with white eyes. Height 6–9 in. (15–23 cm). Planting distance 12–15 in. (30–38 cm).

Glechoma

G. hederacea (*Nepeta hederacea*) 'Variegata'. Evergreen carpeting perennial with rounded green white-splashed leaves and lavender-blue flowers in spring. Variegated form of ground ivy – a rampageous weed – and less vigorous, needing some weeding in first year or two. Useful in shade. Height 3–4 in. (8–10 cm). Planting distance 18–24 in. (46–60 cm).

Hebe (see also p.222)

H. chathamica. Evergreen carpeting shrub with green foliage and white or violet-tinged flowers in June. Prostrate branches spreading rapidly and rooting. Sun and well-drained soil. Height

4–6 in. (10–15 cm). Planting distance 18–24 in. (46–60 cm).

Lamium

L. maculatum. Evergreen perennial carpeter with dark green white-striped leaves and magenta, pink or white flowers in early summer. Will thrive in deep shade. Height 3–4 in. (8—10 cm). Planting distance 12–15 in. (30–38 cm).

Luzula

L. maxima (*L. sylvatica*), woodrush. Evergreen colonising grass, spreading quickly to form solid mats. Rampant but ideal for dense dry shade, steep banks and other difficult places. 'Variegata' has cream-edged leaves and is slightly less invasive. Height 12 in. (30 cm). Planting distance 12–15 in. (30–38 cm).

Lysimachia

L. nummularia, creeping Jenny. Evergreen carpeting perennial with bright green rounded leaves and yellow flowers in summer. Moist sites in sun or shade. Needs weeding in first year. 'Aurea' has golden leaves but may be scorched in sun. Height 1–2 in. (2–5 cm). Planting distance 12–15 in. (30–38 cm).

Maiaenthemum

M. bifolium. Deciduous perennial coloniser with smooth green leaves and creamy white flowers in late spring. Cool soil with leaf-mould, in shade. Height 4–5 in. (10–13 cm). Planting distance 12–15 in. (30–38 cm).

Meuhlenbeckia

M. axillaris. Deciduous colonising shrub with tiny round leaves and minute pale green flowers in July. Threadlike stems develop into a tangled mass and can smother small plants. Best in full sun. Height 6–9 in. (15–23 cm). Planting distance 18 in. (46 cm).

Omphalodes

O. cappodocica. Deciduous colonising perennial with glossy leaves and blue flowers in early summer. Best in shade and rich soil but withstands sun given moist conditions. *O. verna* is smaller. Height 6 in. (15 cm). Planting distance 12 in. (30 cm).

241

Oxalis

O. oregana. Deciduous colonising perennial with rich green clover leaves and white to purplish pink flowers in spring. Fairly dense summer cover in leafy woodland soil and tolerant of deep shade. Increases from rhizomes but not as invasive as *O. acetosella*, wood sorrel, or *O. rubra*.

Phlox

P. subulata and *P. douglasii* hybrids. Deciduous perennial carpeters with needle-like foliage and flowers ranging from violet to pink and white in late spring. 'Temiscaming', magenta, 'May Snow', white, 'Chattahoochee', lavender-blue, and many others can be recommended. Full sun and good drainage. Height 3–4 in. (8–10 cm). Planting distance 9–12 in. (23–30 cm).

Polygonum (knotweed) (see also p.234)

Deciduous carpeting perennials with narrow bright green leaves and erect spikes of pink flowers.
P. affine. 'Darjeeling Red' and 'Superbum' are reliable, bearing richly coloured flowers in summer. 'Donald Lowndes' tends to die out in patches. Sun or light shade, preferably in moist soil. Height 2–3 in. (5–8 cm). Planting distance 9–12 in. (23–30 cm).
P. vacciniifolium. Valuable for late summer flowering. Sometimes slow to establish but then makes dense cover. Open sunny position. Height 3–4 in. (8–10 cm). Planting distance 9–12 in. (23–30 cm).

Potentilla (see also p.227)

Deciduous carpeting perennials for well-drained soils.
P. alba. Leaves green above, grey below, and white orange-centred flowers in spring and autumn. Will accept some shade. Dense when established. Height 2–3 in. (5–8 cm). Planting distance 9–12 in. (23–30 cm).
P. argentea. Similar leaves and sulphur-yellow flowers in spring and autumn. Needs sun. May die back in patches in winter. Height 2–3 in. (5–8 cm). Planting distance 9–12 in. (23–30 cm).

Prunella

P. grandiflora. Evergreen perennial carpeter with hairy dark green leaves and pink or white flowers in July. 'Loveliness' has

242

Rubus tricolor will send out its long trailing stems in the shadiest places, even under beech trees

---

rich pink flowers. Sun or partial shade. Not for dry sandy soil. Height 3–4 in. (8–10 cm). Planting distance 12 in. (30 cm).

Rubus

Evergreen carpeting shrubs related to blackberry, with small white flowers in summer, followed by red fruits. Succeeding in sun or deep shade, in all but poorly drained soils.
R. calycinoides. Wrinkled three-lobed dark green leaves. Prostrate and spreading, making firmly matted cover. Height 2—3 in. (5–8 cm). Planting distance 12–15 in. (30–38 cm).
R. tricolor. Heart-shaped leaves and very bristly stems. Grows strongly but needs weeding at first. Height 12 in. (30 cm). Planting distance 36–38 in. (90–120 cm).

Sarcococca

S. humilis. Evergreen colonising shrub with small glossy green foliage, fragrant white flowers in February and black fruits. Neat dense habit, increasing by suckers to form clumps. Likes a shady position in leaf-enriched soil. Height 9–15 in. (23–38 cm). Planting distance 12–15 in. (30–38 cm).

Saxifraga (saxifrage)

Mossy hybrids. Evergreen perennial carpeters with fresh green

243

Left: The mossy saxifrages, such as 'Four Winds', grow into large rounded cushions
Right: The dainty *Stephanandra incisa* 'Crispa' may be pruned in March to keep it tidy

leaves, sometimes bronze or grey, and flowers from white to deep red in early summer. Usually make thick mats or mounds of foliage. Best in well-drained soil in cool, slightly shady situation. Height 2–3 in. (5–8 cm). Planting distance 12 in. (30 cm).

Sedum (stonecrop)

Evergreen carpeting perennials with smooth fleshy leaves and heads of starry flowers in summer. Sun and reasonable drainage, thriving in poor soil.
S. *spathulifolium*. Purplish or greyish white leaves and tiny yellow flowers. S. *spurium* has green leaves and pink flowers. 'Green Mantle' is non-flowering and an excellent carpeter. Height 2–3 in. (5–8 cm). Planting distance 9–12 in. (23–30 cm)

Stachys

S. *olympica* 'Silver Carpet'. Evergreen perennial carpeter with velvety silver foliage. Non-flowering form of lamb's ears. Sun and well-drained soil. Height 3–4 in. (8–10 cm). Planting distance 12–15 in. (30–38 cm). (See p.196.)

Stephanandra

S. *incisa* 'Crispa'. Deciduous carpeting shrub with deeply incised fresh green leaves, crisped when young and turning orange in autumn. Forms a low network of arching branches. Any but very dry soils in sun or slight shade. Height 18–24 in. (46–60 cm). Planting distance 36 in. (90 cm).

Symphoricarpos

S. × *chenaultii* 'Hancock'. Deciduous colonising and carpeting shrub with pink fruits in autumn. Makes mounds of arching branches. Almost any situation, though thinner in shade. Height 18–24 in. (46–60 cm). Planting distance 36 in. (90 cm).

Symphytum (comfrey)

S. *grandiflorum*. Deciduous carpeting and colonising perennial with broad hairy leaves and creamy bell flowers in spring. 'Hidcote Pink' and 'Hidcote Blue' are taller. Excellent and rapid cover under trees and shrubs, preferably in moist soil. Height 6 in. (15 cm). Planting distance 12 in. (30 cm).

Tellima

T. *grandiflora*. Evergreen perennial carpeter with rounded green leaves becoming bronzed in winter and sprays of creamy flowers in late spring. 'Purpurea' has foliage turning purplish in winter and pinkish flowers. Sun or shade in any except poorly drained soils. Height 6 in. (15 cm). Planting distance 12 in. (30 cm).

Thymus (thyme)

T. *serpyllum*. Evergreen carpeting shrub with tiny dark green leaves on trailing stems and dense rounded heads of rosy purple flowers in summer. Forms available with white, lilac or pink flowers, including 'Pink Chintz'. Full sun and good drainage. Height 1 in. (2 cm). Planting distance 9 in. (23 cm).

Tiarella

T. *cordifolia*, foam flower. Evergreen carpeting perennial with rich green leaves, bronze-tinted in winter, and a froth of creamy white flowers in spring. T. *wherryi* has pinkish white flowers but is slower. Leaf-enriched soil in shade. Height 3–4 in. (8–10 cm). Planting distance 12–15 in. (30–38 cm). (See p.197.)

Vaccinium

V. *vitis-idaea*, cowberry. Evergreen colonising shrub with box-like shiny green leaves, burnished in winter, and white or pinkish bell flowers in summer, following by dark red berries. Acid humus-enriched soil and shade. Height 6 in. (15 cm). Planting distance 9–12 in. (23–30 cm).

Vancouveria

V. hexandra. Deciduous colonising perennial with divided foliage and sprays of white flowers in spring, similar to *Epimedium* (p.238). Best in shade and fairly rich soil. Will tolerate open position but less vigorous. Height 6 in. (15 cm). Planting distance 12 in. (30 cm).

Veronica

V. prostrata. Evergreen perennial carpeter forming mats of prostrate stems, with dense clusters of deep blue flowers in May and June. 'Kapitan' and 'Spode Blue' are good forms. Sun and well-drained soil. Height 1–2 in. (2–5 cm). Planting distance 9–12 in. (23–30 cm).

Viola

Useful perennials for any well-drained soil and tolerant of shade. Height 3–4 in. (8–10 cm). Planting distance 9–12 in. (23–30 cm). *V. cornuta.* Evergreen carpeter with thick light green foliage and masses of lilac-purple or white flowers in summer. Succeeds in

Viola 'Huntercombe Purple' can be cut over after blooming to encourage further flowers

cool open situation with good drainage. V. 'Huntercombe Purple' has rich purple flowers and enjoys the same conditions. Other equally effective forms are 'Haslemere', lavender-pink, 'Connie', white, and 'Martin', deep purple.

V. labradorica. Evergreen coloniser with purple-flushed foliage and lavender-blue violet flowers in spring. Good in dense shade or sun. Runs freely underground and can become a nuisance. (See p.197.)

V. obliqua (V. cucullata). Deciduous coloniser with foliage slowly forming compact mats to give dense summer cover and bearing purple or white flowers in early summer. Good in any but boggy soils and in dense shade.

OTHERS

Clematis

C. orientalis. Deciduous climbing shrub with twining leaf stalks and yellow bell flowers in late summer and autumn. Grows rapidly to give dense tangled mass of growth in sun or moderate shade and any reasonable soil. Good for banks. Height 24 in. (60 cm). Planting distance 6 ft (1.8 m).

Lonicera (see also p.225)

L. japonica var. halliana. Evergreen climbing shrub with twining stems and fragrant honeysuckle flowers, white then yellow, from July onwards. Very vigorous, often rooting as it sprawls, and quickly making a dense canopy. Only for large areas where it cannot strangle other plants. Sun or shade. L. henryi has purplish red flowers in midsummer and may be used in the same way. Height 12 in. (30 cm). Planting distance 36 in. (90 cm).

Rhododendron

Hummock-forming, sometimes carpeting or colonising, evergreen shrubs, with beautiful flowers from spring to summer and often with attractive foliage. Slow-growing but eventually achieving good cover. Acid woodland conditions in humus-enriched soil. Many species and hybrids are suitable, as are some Japanese azaleas. (For further details, see the Wisley Handbook, Rhododendrons.)

Rosa (rose)

Only a few roses are really effective and these will give thick cover, although requiring weeding for the first two seasons after

The widespreading, prickly *Rosa* 'Max Graf' is only suitable for larger gardens

planting. Low-growing shrub roses, such as 'Bonica', 'Ferdy', 'Rosy Cushion' and 'Smarty', are particularly suitable for smaller gardens, growing about 36 in. (90 cm) high and 48 in. (120 cm) across. Full sun.

R. × *paulii*. Deciduous hummock-former, making a dense mound of very prickly interlacing branches with clusters of starry white scented flowers in midsummer. Far-spreading but useful for banks and large areas. Height 5 ft (1.5 m). Planting distance 15 ft (4.5 m).

R. wichuraiana. Carpeting rambler rose, evergreen or deciduous, with smooth dark green leaves and very fragrant white flowers in August and later. Very low, with almost thornless trails developing up to 10 ft (3 m) in a season and eventually spreading far. 'Max Graf' is a slightly taller evergreen hybrid with bright pink flowers in summer. More modern hybrids are 'Pheasant', 'Partridge', and 'Grouse'. 'Temple Bells' has white flowers and at Wisley has fully covered the ground in two seasons, planted 36–48 in. (90–120 cm) apart. Height 18 in. (46 cm). Planting distance 8 ft (2.5 m).

Above: Candytuft, *Iberis sempervirens*, is an old favourite in gardens
Below: The flowers of *Hosta rectifolia* 'Tall Boy' add to its attractions as a foliage plant

Index

Figures in **bold** type refer to illustrations